D1034155

ON WAGES AND COMBINATION

Also by ROBERT TORRENS

In REPRINTS OF ECONOMIC CLASSICS

The Budget [1844]

An Essay on the External Corn Trade [1815]

An Essay on the Production of Wealth [1821]

ON

WAGES

AND

COMBINATION

BY

ROBERT TORRENS

[1834]

REPRINTS OF ECONOMIC CLASSICS

Augustus M. Kelley · Publishers
NEW YORK 1969

First Edition 1834

(London: Longman, Rees, Orme, Brown, Green &
Longman, *Paternoster Row*, 1834)

Reprinted 1969 by

AUGUSTUS M. KELLEY · PUBLISHERS

New York   New York   10001

. . . .

S B N 678-00577-X

L C N 73-95604

. . . .

PRINTED IN THE UNITED STATES OF AMERICA
by SENTRY PRESS, NEW YORK, N. Y. 10019

ON

WAGES AND COMBINATION.

ON

WAGES AND COMBINATION.

BY

R. TORRENS, Esq. M.P. F.R.S.

LONDON:

LONGMAN, REES, ORME, BROWN, GREEN, & LONGMAN,
PATERNOSTER ROW.

1834.

ELECTORS AND INHABITANTS

OF

BOLTON.

———◆———

GENTLEMEN,

I HAVE been, for some time, engaged in preparing an extensive work upon the financial and commercial resources of the country. This work contains some chapters upon wages, and upon the effects of combinations for regulating them, which appear peculiarly applicable at the present crisis ; and, therefore, without waiting for the more general work, of which they form a component part, I publish them in a detached and separate form.

To the Inhabitants of Bolton, it is of paramount importance, that wages should be permanently high. The great majority of the people, whose only source of income is their labour, have a direct and immediate interest in obtaining for that labour the greatest possible reward; the house keepers who engage in the local trade of the district, have a more indirect, but a not less certain interest in high wages, inasmuch as, with the increase in the labourers' means of purchasing, their business and their profits must increase also; and the proprietors of houses, of cottages, and of building ground, have an interest in high wages, because, in proportion to the general prosperity, the demand for tenements will increase, and rents will improve, and be more punctually paid. Thus, it is the universal interest of the town, that labour should obtain an ample reward; and, as the representative of that universal interest, I have felt it to be my duty to endeavour to ascertain, upon what principles, and to what extent, it is practicable to increase wages.

Bolton has had the honour of originating some of the most important improvements in the great staple manufacture of England; and I trust that it is destined to have the further honour, of setting an enlightened example, of the manner in which those improvements may be rendered most conducive to the prosperity of the country, and to the permanent comfort and happiness of the people.

With these views I request permission, to dedicate the following pages to you, as a testimony of my sincere respect, and as a memorial of the enduring gratitude I feel, for the proud distinction which your partial favour has conferred upon me.

I have the honor to be,

GENTLEMEN,

Your faithful Servant, and

very sincere Friend,

R. TORRENS.

CONTENTS.

———◆———

Page

WAGES AND COMBINATION.

————◆————

CHAPTER I.

ON THE GENERAL PRINCIPLES WHICH REGULATE WAGES.

THE principles which regulate the wages of labour form, without any exception, the most interesting and the most important division of Political Economy. The labouring classes compose the great bulk of every community; and a country is happy or miserable, as they are well or ill supplied with the necessaries, comforts, and enjoyments of life. The study of Political Economy, if it did not teach the way in which labour may obtain an adequate reward, might serve to gratify a merely speculative curiosity, but could scarcely conduce to any purposes of practical utility. It claims the peculiar attention of the benevolent and good, mainly because it explains the causes, which depress and elevate wages, and thereby points out the means, by which we may mitigate the distress, and improve the condition, of the great majority of mankind. Political Economy is not, as has been erroneously stated, the appropriate science of the statesman and the legislator ; it is peculiarly and emphatically, *the science of the people.*

Definition of the Term Labour.

To many of our readers it may be matter of surprise that we should deem it necessary to give a formal definition of a word so simple, and so generally understood, as the term labour. The fact is, that recent economical writers, of no inconsiderable eminence, have employed their terms in so many different senses, and extended their signification to so many dissimilar things, that the language of the science has been rendered loose and indeterminate; and that, in using the most familiar words, it often becomes necessary, not only to explain what their meaning *is*, but to point out *what it is not.*

Our first parents, even before the condemnation to " eat by the sweat of their brow," could not have brought the fruits of Eden to their lips by a thought, or a wish; they must have employed some degree of muscular or manual exertion, in order to gather them. Now muscular, or manual exertion, employed in order to procure the objects of desire, is that which, in the language of Political Economy, we denominate labour.

Mental exertion, when employed, as it often is,

in procuring for us the objects of our desire, is called mental, or intellectual labour. Whenever the term is used without such qualifying epithets, it means human muscular exertion, *and nothing more.*

In the production of wealth, the agency of the inferior animals, the agency of machines, and the agency of the powers of nature, are frequently employed to produce effects similar to those, which are produced by human agency. But it is not, therefore, correct to speak, as some economical writers do*, of the labour of cattle, the labour of machines, and the labour of nature. In the language of Political Economy, every thing should be precise and definite; and our terms, instead of being *generalized,* so as to confound distinctions, should be *particularized,* so as to mark the shades of difference between analogous objects—and to place them before us separate, and, as it were, at a distance from each other. Instead of applying the same common term to the several agencies of men, of cattle, of machines, and of nature—we should say the *labour* of men, the *work* of cattle, the *action* of machines, and the *operations* of nature.

It is sometimes said, that " in the idea of labour, the idea of subsistence is included†;" and that " when we speak of labour as *a thing by itself,* the idea of subsistence is included in it." Such

* M'Culloch.   † Mill.

loose modes of expression are, to say the least of them, neither very logical, nor very intelligible.

Labour is one thing; the subsistence which supports the labourer is another, and a very different thing ; and confounding these two different things under one common term, can only lead to ambiguity, misconception, and error. To say, that, when we consider labour as *a thing by itself,* we include in the consideration another and a different thing, is manifestly absurd and contradictory.

In the writings of political economists, we frequently meet with the phrases " accumulated labour," " hoarded labour." These forms of expression are incorrect. We may accumulate and hoard the articles which labour has produced ; but the labour itself, the action of the human muscles, ceased to exist the instant it was performed, and became, in the nature of things, incapable of being either accumulated or hoarded. " Accumulated labour," and " hoarded labour," are, at the best, but figurative expressions, not of the happiest kind ; and to introduce them into the precise and accurate discussions of Political Economy, is to substitute the diction of poetry for the nomenclature of science.

The term labour, then, when its meaning is unqualified by the epithet " mental," or " intellectual," signifies the action of the human muscles, directed to obtain the objects of desire ; and it signifies *nothing more.*

Definition of Wages.

When men cease to work upon their own account, they must receive from their employers, in exchange for their labour, such articles of wealth, as may be necessary to preserve them in working condition, and to enable them to keep up the race of labourers. The articles of wealth which the labourer receives, in exchange for his labour, are denominated wages. When the quantity of necessaries and comforts which the labourer receives is large, wages are said to be high; when it is small, they are said to be low.

When money becomes the instrument of exchanging one thing for another, a distinction must be made between money wages, and commodity wages; or, in other words, between nominal and real wages. Real wages consist of the *quantity* of necessaries and comforts which the labourer receives; nominal wages of the *sum of money*, in which he is paid. If money always retained the same value, in relation to the necessaries and comforts of life, nominal wages would always be a correct measure of real wages; and both would rise or fall together, and in the same proportion. But the exchangeable power of money is liable to constant fluctuations, and therefore nominal wages often rise while real wages fall, and fall while real wages rise. It is almost superfluous to add, that it is on the state, not of nominal, but of real wages, that the condition of the working classes depends.

It is sometimes said that wages rise and fall, not as the labourer receives a greater or a less *quantity* of wealth* ; but, on the contrary, as he receives a greater or a less *proportion* of the whole wealth produced. Thus, if the labourer had received, as his annual wages, fifty quarters of corn and fifty suits of clothing, when the whole annual produce of his labour was one hundred quarters and one hundred suits; then, if he should receive only twenty-five quarters and twenty-five suits when the whole produce of his labour became only forty quarters and forty suits, his wages, instead of having fallen one-half, would have experienced a considerable rise ; because the proportion of twenty-five to forty-five is greater than the proportion of fifty to one hundred. In this sense of the terms, wages may be falling while the labourer is earning a more abundant quantity of all the necessaries and comforts of life ; and may be rising, while he is sinking to a state of the utmost destitution, and actually perishing of famine. This is a strange and unnecessary, not to say absurd, perversion of language.

The term wages is sometimes employed in a very extensive sense, being made to signify not only that which is given to the labourer, but all the other advances of the capitalist. This generalization is improper. The term *capital* is the general term, comprising that which is given to

---

* Ricardo, M'Culloch, Mill.

the labourer, and that which s advanced as seed, material, and machinery; the term wages is the specific term, marking that particular portion of the capitalist's advances which is given to the labourer for his labour. When we extend the signification of the term wages to seed, material, and machinery, we render it synonimous with the term capital. For the sake of convenience and precision, it is necessary that some one term should be appropriated to signify that particular portion of capital which is advanced directly and immediately to the labourer, in payment for his labour ; and the term which general usage has so appropriated is—wages. To call seed, material, and machinery, *wages,* is a confounding of terms : to call them the wages of that non-entity, accumulated labour, is still worse. Such vague generalization involves us in endless ambiguity, obscurity, and confusion. In the vocabulary of Political Economy, as in the language of common life, the term wages signifies that which is paid for labour, and signifies *nothing more.*

The Maximum of Wages.

As wages are paid out of the produce of industry, it is obvious that there are natural and necessary limits, beyond which they cannot be permanently increased. Thus, if 100 labourers expend 200 quarters of corn for seed and implements, and raise a return of 500 quarters, it is physically impossible that their wages should continue to be more than 300 quarters; because, if they did, seed and implements would not be replaced, and the capitalists could not continue the cultivation of the earth. Again, if it were necessary to resort to an inferior soil, upon which 100 labourers, with an expenditure of 200 quarters for seed and implements, could raise no more than 400 quarters, then, for the same reason, it would become physically impossible that the annual wages of 100 men should exceed 200 quarters of corn.

In the above cases, the labourer is supposed to receive as his wages the whole produce of labour, which remains after the replacement of the capitalist's other advances. This can occur only in those rare instances in which the capitalist, without seeking any profit for himself, employs labourers from pure benevolence and charity. In the vast majority of actual cases, the capitalist, in addition to the replacement of all his advances, will reserve a portion of the produce of industry as his profit; and though there will exist no physical, yet there will be a moral impossibility, that wages should exceed that, which remains after the capitalist's other advances have been replaced, with the lowest rate of increase, for the sake of which he will carry on his business. This, then, we may call the *moral maximum* of wages. The labourer may receive more, as a benevolent gift, from men of fortune, who do not live upon their industry; but he cannot receive more, in exchange for common labour, in those great and permanent branches of employment which supply the community with the necessaries and comforts of life.

The rate of increase, which is sufficient to induce the capitalist to continue in business, varies, from causes, which it is not necessary here to explain. We may for the present safely assume, that the capitalist will not engage in the work of production, unless he can obtain a profit of seven per cent.

If we take seven per cent. as the lowest rate of profit, then the maximum, beyond which wages cannot rise, will be that portion of the produce, which remains, after replacing the advances not consisting of wages, and deducting what is equivalent to seven per cent. upon the whole advances. Thus, if a farmer advance to 100 labourers 200 quarters of corn, as wages, with 200 quarters more for seed and implements; and if he obtain a return of 428 quarters, wages will be at the maximum, for, if we take from the whole produce of 428 quarters, 200 quarters, to replace the seed and implements consumed, and also deduct 28 quarters, or seven per cent., upon the whole advance of 400 quarters, then just 200 quarters will remain to be again advanced as wages. Under these circumstances, it is self-evident that wages could not rise above 200 quarters for 100 men, for were more than this given to the labourers, too little would remain, either for seeds and implements, or for that lowest rate of profit which will induce the farmer to cultivate.

It is obvious, that the maximum of wages may
be raised, either by the cultivation of land of a
better quality, or by improvements in the effective
powers of industry; and that it may be lowered,
either by resorting to poorer soils, or by a falling
off in the effective powers of industry. In an
improving country, better modes of culture are
gradually introduced, and labour is more effectually applied, particularly in manufactures. But
the effect of such improvements, in raising the
maximum of wages, is in general counterbalanced
by the necessity of resorting to inferior, or more
distant soils for the supply of food and material.

The circumstances, which raise the maximum
of wages to the highest point, are those in which
a thickly-peopled country, excelling in manufacturing industry, carries on a perfectly free trade
with thinly-peopled countries, in which none but
soils of first-rate quality are under tillage. A
simple illustration will demonstrate this.

If a master manufacturer employ 100 labourers,
who fabricate for him 428 suits of clothing, and if,
from the inferior quality of the soil under cultivation, he is obliged to give 200 suits for the
materials he works up, it is evident that the
highest point to which the wages of the 100
labourers can ascend will be 200 suits of clothing;
because if more were given for labour, the capitalist
would have less than the lowest rate of profit,
which is necessary to induce him to continue in
business.

Now, let an unrestricted commerce in agri-

cultural produce be established with a new country, cultivating none but first-rate soils, and let
raw produce be in consequence so reduced in value
—as compared with wrought goods, that the
manufacturer can purchase his raw material for
100, instead of for 200 suits of clothing; and
immediately the maximum of wages, for the 100
labourers, will rise from 200 to 300 suits—because
the capitalist, obtaining 428 suits, and advancing
only 100 for materials, may give 300 to his labourers,
and yet retain 28 suits, or seven per cent. upon his
whole advance of 400 suits. Measured in clothing,
maximum wages will have risen 50 per cent.,
measured in raw produce they will appear to have
risen 300 per cent.

England having acquired in manufacturing industry an efficacy unexampled in the history of
the world, and having the new countries of the
American continent open to her commerce, is
placed in that precise situation, in which the
maximum of wages may be elevated to the highest
attainable point. But the vast, the incalculable
advantages of this situation are counteracted by
the restrictive system, which excludes cheap raw
produce from our markets.

The Minimum of Wages.

The mininum below which wages cannot permanently fall, consists in a quantity of the necessaries and conveniences of life sufficient to preserve
the labourer in working condition, and to induce

him to keep up the race of labourers. The point, below which wages cannot fall, is not a fixed and immutable point, but is, on the contrary, liable to considerable variation. The shelter and clothing indispensable in one country may be unnecessary in another. A labourer in Hindostan may continue to work with perfect vigour, while receiving a supply of clothing which would be insufficient to preserve a labourer in Russia from perishing. Even in countries, situate in the same climate, different habits of living will often occasion variations in the minimum of wages, as considerable as those which are produced by natural causes.

The labourer in Ireland will rear a family under circumstances which would not only deter an English workman from marriage, but would force him on the parish for personal support. Now, it is certain, that a gradual introduction of capital into Ireland, accompanied by such a diffusion of instruction amongst the people, as would impart to them a taste for the comforts of life, might raise the minimum of wages in that country to an equality with their minimum in England; and we can conceive a succession of impoverishing and calamitous causes, which might so reduce the spirit of the people of England, as to render them satisfied with the scanty pittance, that the labourer obtains in the sister island. Alterations, however, in the minimum of wages cannot be suddenly effected. So far as this minimum depends upon climate, it is unchangeable; and even so far as it is determined by the habits of living, and the established scale of comfort, it can be effected only by those circumstances of prosperity or decay, and by those moral causes of instruction and civilization, which are ever gradual in their operation. The minimum of wages, therefore, though it varies under different climates, and with the different stages of national improvement, may, in any given time and place, be regarded as very nearly stationary.

On the circumstances, which determine the point, at which actual Wages settle.

We have seen, that the *minimum* of wages is that quantity of the products, of industry, which climate and custom render necessary, in order to support the labourer while at work, and to induce him to keep up the race of labourers ; and it has appeared that the *maximum* of wages is that quantity of the products of industry which remains, after replacing the advances, not consisting of wages, and paying the capitalist the lowest rate of profit, which will induce him to continue the work of production.

Now, when climate and custom have fixed the minimum, below which the reward of labour cannot fall, and when the quality of the soil, the skill with which labour is applied, and the degree of freedom which is allowed to trade, have determined the maximum, beyond which it cannot rise,

what is the precise circumstance which fixes the
point at which actual wages settle?

In order to put this important question in a
more exact and definite form, we will assume that
the minimum wages of the labourer are five
quarters of corn a year; and that the minimum
profit, for the sake of which the capitalist will
make advances, is seven per cent.; and we will
suppose that a farmer, by employing 100 labourers,
and advancing 500 quarters of corn for seed
and implements, obtains a reproduction of 1605
quarters. In this case, what is to determine the
wages which the 100 labourers shall receive?
They may receive only 500 quarters, should wages
fall to the minimum; or they may receive 1000
quarters, should wages rise to the maximum;
because, as the farmer obtains a reproduction of
1605 quarters, he may, in addition to his advance
of 500 quarters for seed and implements, pay 1000
quarters to his 100 labourers, and still have, upon
this whole advance of 1500 quarters, the minimum
profit of seven per cent., which is sufficient to
induce him to continue his business. What then
determines whether the 100 labourers shall receive
as their wages 500 quarters or 1000 quarters,
or some medium quantity between these two
extremes?

The answer to this question is, that the one and
the only cause which can determine where, between
the maximum and minimum, the wages of these

100 labourers shall be fixed, is, the proportion between the number of labourers and the quantity of that component part of our farmer's capital, which he can exchange for labour. A mere statement of the relation between the amount of the capital and the quantity of the labour will render this self-evident.

How the proportion between Capital and Labour regulates actual Wages.

The farmer, on commencing business, commands, we will say, a capital of 1000 quarters of corn ; 500 quarters of which he advances for seed and implements. Over and above his necessary expenditure for these component parts of agricultural capital, he has but 500 quarters disposable ; and therefore it is physically impossible that he should give to his 100 labourers more than those 500 quarters as their wages.

The farmer obtains a reproduction of 1605 quarters; but if 605 quarters of these are absorbed in the current expenses of his family, his capital, at the commencement of the second year, will remain exactly the same as it was at the commencement of the first, and any increase of wages will continue to be impossible.

But supposing that our farmer, out of the 605 quarters formerly devoted to the current expenses of his family, contrives to save 250 quarters, and adds them to his capital of 1000 quarters, then it will immediately become possible for an advance of wages to take place ; and assuming that the number of labourers remain as before, an advance of wages equal to the increase of capital necessarily will take place ; the 100 labourers receiving 725 quarters instead of 500 quarters. For when the farmer, in order to extend his cultivation, makes an addition to his capital, he will require a greater number of hands, and will seek to tempt them into his employ by the offer of higher wages. But as the increase of capital is supposed to be general, all other capitalists will require additional hands as well as our farmer, and will be offering higher wages also. All the capitalists will be unwilling to let their additional capital lie idle for want of hands, and, with the two-fold object of retaining their own labourers, and of obtaining those of their neighbours, will go on advancing wages, until the whole of their additional capital is absorbed.

Assuming that all the labourers are already employed, and that no addition is made to their numbers, it is morally certain, that the whole of every new accumulation of capital will assume the form of increased wages, until the reward of the labourer has reached its maximum. New accumulations of capital are made for the sake of obtaining advantage therefrom. But it is impossible that new accumulations of capital should be advantageously employed, unless labourers can be procured. The new capital, accumulated for the purpose of gaining an advantage by the employ-

ment of labourers, comes into the market and bids
for hands; the old capital, in order to retain its
hands, is compelled to bid against the new, and
this process goes on until the whole existing capital is invested in wages, seed, materials, and
machinery. But as a given number of hands can
use only a given quantity of seed, materials,
and machinery, these ingredients or component
parts of capital cannot be increased, while the
quantity of labour remains the same; and therefore it is only in the form of increased wages that
the new accumulations of capital can appear.

When the number of labourers remains the same,
nothing can prevent new accumulations of capital
from appearing under the form of increased wages,
except such an intimate understanding and concert
amongst capitalists, as would induce each individual
of the class, instead of seeking for additional hands,
to allow all his new accumulations of capital to
remain idle and unproductive. But the supposition of an intimate concert amongst capitalists, for
such a purpose, involves this manifest contradiction
and absurdity — namely, that they accumulate
capital for the sake of employing it advantageously,
at the same time that they resolve not to employ
it at all. If there were an understanding that all
new capital should be kept unemployed, no new
accumulation would take place. Whenever new
accumulations do take place, they supply a complete demonstration that no combination for the
purpose of not employing them exists. If such

new accumulations are made, it is in order that they may be employed; and if they are employed the quantity of labour, and the state of knowledge in applying mechanical power remaining the same, there is no form in which they can appear, except in that of increased wages.

On this principle, if our farmer, employing as before, 100 labourers, advancing 500 quarters of corn as seed and implements, and obtaining a reproduction of 1605 quarters, were, out of the 605 quarters formerly devoted to the current expenses of his family, to save 500 quarters instead of 250 quarters, then the second 250 quarters, thereby added to his capital, would, like the first, take the form of increased wages, and the reward of the 100 labourers, which had before risen from 500 to 750 quarters, would now rise to 1000 quarters. Here wages would have reached their maximum; for the farmer, advancing 500 quarters for seed, and 1000 quarters for labour, and obtaining a reproduction of 1605 quarters, would gain no more than the minimum profit of seven per cent., which, by the supposition, is necessary, to induce him to carry on his business.

Under these circumstances, it is plain that if the number of labourers did not increase, wages would continue at their maximum. Should the labouring class, during the increase of capital and advance of wages, have acquired a taste for superior modes of living, the minimum, below which wages cannot fall without reducing the supply of labour, might be made to coincide with the maximum, beyond which they cannot rise without suspending the employment of capital. When the coincidence of minimum and maximum wages is brought about by superior habits of living among the people, raising the former to the level of the latter, the labouring classes will be in the most affluent condition in which, in the nature of things, it is possible they should be placed.

This affluent condition can be preserved to the labouring classes so long only as they may refuse to burthen themselves with families sufficient to keep up the race, unless they receive the highest wages which can be paid, without trenching upon the minimum rate of profit. An increase in the number of labourers, without a contemporaneous and proportional increase in the quantity of those ingredients of capital by which labour is, maintained, is inevitably followed by a decline of wages. While our farmer's capital consists of seed and implements sufficient to employ 100 labourers, and of a quantity of necessaries sufficient to pay them wages, at the rate of 10 quarters of corn per man, it is physically impossible that he should, with this capital, give employment to 110 labourers at the same wages.

It necessarily follows, from the principles of rent, that when, on the last land resorted to, the smallness of the produce obtained, deprives the farmer of the power of giving his labourers more than is sufficient for the support of animal life, the high rent which competition causes to be paid for all the more fertile soils, reduces the cultivator of the best to the same level with the cultivator of the worst, and brings down universally the maximum of wages to the minimum.

Hitherto we have taken our proofs and illustrations from agricultural labour, because in agriculture the principal things expended, such as food and seed, being homogeneous with the things reproduced, we are enabled to form a direct comparison between the quantities expended and the quantities reproduced, and thus to give a simplicity and distinctness to our illustrations, which could not otherwise be obtained. The principles, however, which regulate wages in agriculture, also regulate them in manufactures. Where, as is now the case in this country, competition is allowed to operate, the value of the common labour employed in producing the first necessaries of life will regulate the value of all other kinds of labour; allowance being made for different degrees of hardship and of hazard, and for the time and expense required in learning a trade.

Beyond a certain point, the proportion between Capital and Labour ceases to have any influence on Wages.

It has appeared that minimum wages are fixed by climate, and by the habits of living prevalent among the labouring classes; that maximum wages are determined by the quality of the soil under cultivation, by the skill with which labour is applied, and by the degree of freedom allowed to trade; and that the point at which actual wages settle is regulated by the proportion which exists between the number of labourers to be maintained, and the quantity of those ingredients of capital which are destined for their maintenance.

The ratio between labour and capital appears sometimes to be considered as the only regulator of wages. If the condition of the great body of the people be easy and comfortable, it is contended that all that is necessary to keep it so is to make capital increase as fast as population; or, on the other hand, to prevent population from increasing faster than capital; and that if the condition of the people be not easy and comfortable, it can be made so only by quickening the rate at which capital increases, or by retarding the rate at which population increases*.

This is taking a narrow and incomplete view of the circumstances which regulate wages. The ratio between labour and capital is not the only cause; it is but one out of the several causes by which wages are governed. When climate and custom have determined the point below which the reward of labour cannot fall, and when the quality of the soil, and the skill with which industry is applied, have fixed the maximum beyond

* Mill.

which it cannot rise, then the ratio between population and capital, or, more correctly, between the quantity of labour and the quantity of the ingredients of capital destined for its maintenance, determines the intermediate point at which actual wages settle. But though labour and capital should go on increasing in the same proportion, and though they should constantly preserve the same ratio to each other, yet the necessity of resorting to inferior soils might gradually reduce the maximum of wages until it coincided with the extreme minimum, below which labour cannot be sustained. At this point the supply of labour could be no further increased ; and if habits of frugality amongst the opulent classes continued to convert revenue into capital, the ratio of capital to population might go on increasing, without producing the slightest advance of wages.

When, in the progress of wealth and population, wages and profits have fallen to their minimum, and when the next quality of land to be taken in cannot be made to yield a reproduction sufficient to pay these minimum wages and to replace advances with minimum profits, then that which is saved from revenue to be added to capital cannot be employed at home, and will be invested in foreign loans and foreign adventures. At this point the most rapid accumulation of capital, though going on while population remained stationary, could have no possible influence on wages.

The means by which Wages may be increased.

The circumstances most favourable to the comfort and happiness of the great body of the people, are those in which the cultivation of none but superior soils, and the divisions of employment, with the aid of machinery, raise the effective powers of industry, and, consequently, the maximum of wages to the highest point; while the rapid increase of capital, or the prudential habits of the people with respect to increasing their numbers, preserves between the quantity of labour and the quantity of those ingredients of capital which are applicable to its support, that proportion which brings actual, up to the level of maximum wages.

The circumstances most unfavourable to the comfort and happiness of the labouring class, are those in which the low effective powers, either of agricultural or of manufacturing industry, bring down the maximum of wages to a level with the extreme minimum, below which the merely animal wants of the labouring population cannot be supplied. Under such circumstances, the condition of the great body of the people is melancholy and calamitous in the highest degree. Already standing on the extreme verge of existence, on every stagnation of trade and deficient harvest, they are deprived of support, and visited by famine.

Should the resorting to soils of an inferior quality, and the low effective powers of agricultural industry consequent thereto, be the cause which brings down the maximum of wages to the level of their extreme minimum, then the degradation and misery of the people cannot be removed, unless the inferior lands are thrown out of cultivation, either by the free importation of foreign agricultural produce, or by such a reduction of the population as may enable the lands of superior quality to yield a sufficient supply of food and material for the numbers which remain.

It is to be carefully remembered, however, that the importation of foreign agricultural produce, and the consequent throwing out of inferior soils, though they will have the effect of raising maximum or possible wages, cannot raise the actual wages received, unless the proportion which the quantity of labour bears to the quantity of the ingredients of capital applicable to its maintenance should be at the same time reduced. If, previous to the importation of foreign corn, 100 labourers, with an expenditure of 500 quarters for seed and implements, could raise 749 quarters from the last quality of soil brought under cultivation, then, minimum profits being seven per cent., the maximum wages of 100 men would be 200 quarters; and if, after the importation of foreign corn, all soils were thrown out of tillage, except those from which 100 labourers, with an expenditure for 500 quarters for seed and implements, could produce 1605 quarters, then the maximum wages of the 100 labourers would rise from 200 quarters to 1000 quarters. But though maximum, or possible wages, might thus advance, it is self-evident that actual wages could not be raised to this maximum, unless the quantity of labour had so diminished, or the amount of capital had so increased, that for every 100 labourers to be employed, the farmer, in addition to his necessary advance for 500 quarters for seed and implements, had 1000 quarters to advance as wages.

It is also to be remembered, that in a country which has approached the ultimate limits of her agricultural resources, and which refuses to admit foreign agricultural produce, a reduction of the population, sufficient to throw the inferior land out of cultivation, though it increases maximum or possible wages, yet will not advance actual wages, if capital should be reduced in the same proportion with population. If the farmer, who employs 100 men, has a capital of only 400 quarters of corn, and if he is obliged to advance 200 quarters for seed and implements, the wages of the 100 men will necessarily be 200 quarters, whether the soil they cultivate yields 428 or 856 quarters. In the former case the farmer's profits will be seven per cent.; in the latter they will be 114 per cent. This very high rate of profit would occasion a rapid increase of capital; and if the population, remaining stationary, rendered it unnecessary again to resort to the inferior land, the wages of the 100 labourers would rise from 200 quarters to 600 quarters, the extreme maximum determined by the superior quality of the soil under cultivation.

From all that has been said, it must be evident that the important power of increasing, or of diminishing, the reward of labour, is, by the essential order of society, placed in the hands of the labourers themselves. Irregularities in the seasons bringing on scarcity and famine, foreign incursions, or domestic commotions, destroying property, or suspending production by rendering it insecure, may sometimes occasion a depression of wages, which no prudence on the part of the labouring classes can avert or mitigate. But under all ordinary circumstances, when the usual course of nature is preserved, and when law and order are maintained, it depends upon the labouring classes themselves whether wages shall ascend to the ultimate maximum, or sink to the extreme minimum. By duly regulating their numbers, in relation to the extent and fertility of the soil, they enlarge the range of maximum wages; and by regulating their numbers, in relation to the component parts of capital employed, they cause actual wages to ascend to their ultimate maximum.

Under such circumstances every improvement in agriculture—every addition to mechanical power —every new facility afforded to communication and transport—every thing, in short, which reduces the cost of bringing the necessaries of life to market, raises, at one and the same time, both possible and actual wages, bestows upon the labouring classes more ample means of comfort and enjoyment, and lifts them to a higher place upon the scale of society.

On the other hand, when the labouring classes allow their numbers to bear a high proportion, either to the extent of fertile land, or to the amount of capital applicable to their maintenance, wages will settle down to the extreme minimum, below which animal existence cannot be sustained. Under such circumstances, every fluctuation of the seasons, every stagnation or revulsion in trade, will bring down upon the labouring population all the miseries of want, and degrade them to a state more precarious and wretched than that of negro servitude.

There is no tendency in Population to increase faster than Capital, and thus to degrade Wages.

Were it true, as has been sometimes stated, that population has a tendency to increase more rapidly than capital*, all endeavours to improve the condition of the people would be completely idle and abortive. The existence of such a tendency would fix the labouring class in a state, not only of hopeless, but of perpetually increasing misery, and would cause in each succeeding year a greater number

* Mill.

to be cut off by famine, and by the epidemics it engenders. The fact, that the condition of the labouring classes has improved with the progress of wealth and civilization, demonstrates that population has not a tendency to increase faster than capital.

Adam Smith has told us, that in the universal opulence of an improving country, the common labourer can command a greater quantity of the necessaries and comforts of life than many an African king, the absolute master of the lives and fortunes of thousands of subject savages. At the present time, a common labourer, in England, is better off, with respect to food, clothing, and furniture, than were the chief men of the land in the days of the Saxon Heptarchy; and many an inhabitant of a work-house is better accommodated now than were the Kings of Britain at the period of the Roman invasion. These facts are totally inconsistent with the supposition, that population has a tendency to increase faster than capital.

The poverty and misery of mankind, in almost all parts of the globe, is no proof that population has a tendency to increase faster than capital has actually increased. To prove the existence of such a tendency, other facts must be supplied. It must be shown, not only that the labouring classes are generally in a state of misery and poverty, but that, from the time that capitalists and labourers became distinct classes, the misery and poverty of the latter has gone on increasing. Even this is not enough. When the fact of the constantly increasing wretchedness of mankind has been established, it is further necessary to show, that the increasing misery has not been produced by another cause, fully adequate to the effect ; namely, by an increase in the ratio of population to the extent of the fertile lands from which erroneous legislation permits subsistence to be obtained.

When we examine this question with the attention and accuracy which its great importance demands, and compare the motives which influence mankind in increasing their numbers, and in accumulating wealth, we find that, in almost every society, the tendency is not to increase population faster than capital ; but, on the contrary, to increase capital more rapidly than population.

In new countries, like North America, where abundance of fertile land remains to be reclaimed, and where the obstacle to production is the want of a population sufficiently dense for the division of employment, and the co-operation of one distinct branch of industry with another, a large family becomes an important source of wealth ; the desire of bettering their condition acts in conjunction with the instinct of nature in impelling the labouring classes to early marriages ; and population increases with as much rapidity as the human constitution will admit. Yet in new countries, where population doubles in the shortest possible period, the accumulation of wealth is at least as rapid ; and capital continues to bear that proportion to labour which makes actual wages permanently high.

In old and well-peopled countries, such as England, the increasing cost of procuring raw produce gives a high value to food, and to those coarse manufactured articles into which raw material largely enters. The high value thus given to the things which constitute real wages, is of no advantage to the married labourer, who must consume, in the maintenance of his family, all the subsistence he receives; but is of great advantage to the unmarried labourer, who, receiving more food and clothing, or the price of more, than he can himself consume, has a surplus quantity, or the price of a surplus quantity, with which to purchase the finer manufactured goods, and the articles of convenience and luxury, which have fallen in value as compared with the necessaries of life. Hence the unmarried labourer finds himself in much more affluent circumstances than the married labourer. While in a new country a numerous family is a powerful means of bettering the condition of the labourer, in an old country, where the produce of the soil has acquired a high value, such a family deprives the working man of the ease, and comfort, and independence which he enjoys in the single state. It follows, that as a country approaches the limits of her agricultural resources, marriages become less frequent; and the *power* " to increase and multiply," instead of being stimulated to its utmost action by the considerations of prudence, and the desire of bettering our condition, is checked and controuled by the prevailing efficacy of these causes to such an extent, that the tendency in every civilized community is not for population to increase faster than capital, but for capital to increase faster than population.

These principles are established by the actual condition of the labouring classes in every country of Europe except Ireland. The strength of the motives by which in an old country the impulse to an increase of numbers is controuled, cannot be sufficiently appreciated, unless we take into our consideration the fact, that these motives have hitherto acted under all the discouragements of erroneous opinion, and mistaken legislation. When the laws which give a bounty to over-population shall be repealed, and when prudence and precaution in entering upon the marriage state, and in limiting the numbers of families, instead of being objects of censure and dislike, receive from the approbation of an enlightened public voice, the reward to which their prevailing influence on human happiness entitles them, then will population be at all times so regulated, that the supply of labour will be duly apportioned to the quantity of fertile land, and to the amount of capital employed ; and the labouring classes will emerge from their degradation, and will permanently enjoy independence and comfort, unaccompanied by the exhaustion of immoderate toil.

The rapidity with which all kinds of useful instruction are at this time spreading amongst the labouring classes of Great Britain would speedily bring about this consummation, so devoutly to be wished, were it not for one most fatal counter-acting cause—the annual inundations of Irish labour. Until this cause is removed, no considerable improvement in the condition of the labouring classes in England and Scotland can, by possibility, take place. Until a taste for a higher scale of comfort becomes prevalent amongst the people of Ireland, no prudential calculations, no desire of lifting themselves from their degradation, will controul the power of increase, and thus raise the reward of their labour to a level with that which is obtained in England. But the two islands are so intimately connected—steam navigation has brought their shores into such immediate contact —that if Irish wages do not rise to the level of English, English wages must fall to the level of Irish.

Let the people of England look to this. Let the labouring classes throughout England and Scotland rest assured, that if effectual means be not applied for improving the habits of their Irish brethren, the political degradation into which they have fallen will, in the re-action of moral causes, sink the great body of the people throughout the United Kingdom to one common level of extreme and hopeless misery.

CHAPTER II.

ON THE EFFECT OF MACHINERY UPON WAGES.

FROM the principles established in the preceding chapter, it must be evident, that in whatever degree the employment of machinery may diminish the cost of production, it must in the same degree raise maximum or possible wages. Assuming, as before, that seven per cent. is the lowest rate of profit, for the sake of which industry will be continued, then if a farmer, employing 100 labourers, with an expenditure of 500 quarters for seed and implements, could raise 749 quarters, the maximum wages of the 100 men, should no rent be paid, would be 200 quarters, or two quarters per man. Now suppose that the farmer, by introducing a threshing machine, a winnowing machine, and a sowing machine, can raise 749 quarters from the land under cultivation, with the labour of 50 instead of 100 men, then it is self-evident that maximum or possible wages will be doubled, and will rise from two quarters to four quarters per man. Before the introduction of these machines, it was physically impossible that any effort of prudence, any diminution of the supply of labour, or any increase in the demand for it, could enable the labourers to earn, as their permanent wages, more than two quarters per man. But, now that the cost of production has been lowered by the employment of machinery, an increase in the demand for labour, or a diminution in its supply, may double wages. A capability of bettering the condition of the working people has been created—the obstacle, formerly insuperable, to their improvement has been removed.

But the practically important questions are— would improvement really take place when it ceased to be impossible? Would *actual* wages rise because *maximum* wages had risen? Let us see.

The employment of the machines has caused an enormous increase in the profits of the farmer. While his produce, equivalent to 749 quarters, remains as before, his expenditure, which was 500 quarters for seed and implements, and 200 quarters for wages for 100 men, is now reduced to 500 quarters for seed and implements, with 100 quarters for wages for 50 men. His profit is, therefore, raised from seven to 24 per cent. Now this increased rate of profit, occasioned by the diminished cost of production, will be followed by an increase in actual, as well as in maximum wages.

The 100 quarters which the farmer formerly paid as wages to 50 men, and which are now added to his profits, he cannot eat, and he will not destroy. He will expend them, either unproductively as revenue, or productively as capital. Should he expend them unproductively, upon an additional quantity of articles of dress and furniture produced within the country, they will go to pay the wages of the additional number of labourers required to fabricate this additional supply of home-made goods. Should he expend them unproductively upon foreign luxuries, they will go to pay the wages of the additional number of labourers, required to produce the additional quantity of home-made goods, with which the additional supply of foreign luxuries must be purchased. In either case, the unproductive expenditure of the 100 quarters, added to the farmer's profits, will create a new demand for labour, exactly equal to the quantity of labour thrown out of employ by the introduction of the machines. The diminished demand for agricultural labour will be balanced by the increased demand for manufacturing labour, and the aggregate demand will remain undiminished. The change of occupation will, in the first instance, be accompanied by considerable local distress ; but after the new proportions, between the agricultural and manufacturing populations, have been adjusted, the same number of labourers will be employed at the same rate of wages as before. On the supposition, therefore, that the farmer expends the whole of his increased profits unproductively, the ultimate effect will be, that maximum wages will be increased, while actual wages will remain unchanged. The quantities of raw materials and food, the funds for employing and maintaining labour, will remain as before; and, should no variation take place in the numbers to be employed and maintained, wages will remain as before.

But when the introduction of the machines increased the farmer's profit from seven to 24 per cent. the whole of this increased profit would not be expended unproductively. Increasing profits always occasion a more rapid accumulation of capital, and an increase of productive expenditure. We have, therefore, to consider what effect would be produced upon actual wages by the more rapid accumulation of capital, and the increased productive expenditure, consequent upon the employment of the machines.

Previous to the employment of the machines, the farmer obtained, from the most inferior soils then under tillage, the rate of profit requisite to induce him to invest capital in cultivation. He can now obtain this rate of profit from lands which could not before be tilled. When the expenditure, upon a given quantity of land, was 700 quarters, the lowest quality of soil which could be cultivated with the minimum profit of seven per cent. must have yielded 749 quarters; now that the machines have reduced the expenditure upon this quantity of land to 600, a quality of soil yielding 642 will afford this rate of profit; a new and extensive field for the employment of accumulating capital will be created; that portion of the farmer's increased profits which he adds to his capital will be employed in bringing additional land into tillage;

an increased quantity of subsistence will be raised ; and, unless the supply of labour should increase in the same proportion, actual wages will advance.

The employment of improved machinery in manufactures would produce precisely similar effects. Let us take the instance of the power-loom, and, for the sake of distinctness, let us trace the result in figures.

A manufacturer's expenditure is, in the first instance, raw material and wear and tear, equivalent to 500 quarters, and wages to 100 hand-loom weavers, equivalent to 200 quarters, and with this expenditure he fabricates cloth equivalent to 749 quarters. He subsequently introduces the power-loom, which, by enabling him to get the same work done by 50 labourers, effects a saving of the wages formerly advanced to the other 50, who are thrown out of employ. The things constituting the wages thus saved, the manufacturer will not destroy— he will advance them either in purchasing, or in producing other things; and in either case, the aggregate quantity of food and clothing appropriated to the maintenance of the labouring classes will suffer no diminution. The new distribution of employment will, for a considerable period, be accompanied by great privation and distress ; but when a sufficient number of the hand-loom weavers, for whose work there is a diminished demand, shall be transferred to those other trades, in which there is an increased demand, there will not be, upon the whole, any reduction in actual wages, even upon the suppo-

sition that the whole saving in the cost of production is expended unproductively, and that no
addition is made to those ingredients of capital
which are applicable to the maintenance of labour.
But this supposition would be contrary to fact.
The saving which the introduction of improved
machinery would effect in the cost of producing
manufactured necessaries, would speedily occasion
an increased creation of the funds applicable to
the maintenance of labour; and, unless a proportional increase should at the same time take place
in the supply of labour, would cause actual wages to
advance. The demand for labour would be rendered either more intense or more extensive, or, in
other words, either the same number of labourers
would be employed at higher wages, or else a
greater number at the same wages. The reduction
in the cost of preparing wrought goods, occasioned
by the employment of machinery in manufactures,
reduces the value of that portion of the farmer's
advances which consists of clothing, furniture, and
implements, and thereby enables him to obtain
additional supplies of food and raw materials, from
tracts which could not formerly be tilled. Let us
take an example.

We will assume that, before the introduction of
improved machinery in manufactures, that part of
the farmer's advances which consists of wrought
goods is of equal value with that part which consists of raw produce. In this case, if he advance
100 quarters as food and seed, he must also advance

clothing, furniture, and implements, equivalent to 100 quarters; and he will be unable to cultivate, with the minimum profit of seven per cent., any land which does not yield to this advance a produce of 214 quarters. Now, let the employment of improved machinery in manufactures diminish by one-half the productive cost, and the value of wrought goods, and the farmer's advance, which was before equivalent to 200 quarters, will now be equivalent only to 150 quarters; and he will be able to cultivate, with the minimum of seven per cent., land yielding only $160\frac{1}{2}$ quarters. Tracts which could not formerly be reclaimed from their original wild and forest state, will now be brought under the plough, and there will not only be a greatly increased demand for agricultural labour, but large additional supplies of food and raw material will be raised, to maintain and employ a more numerous manufacturing population.

Machines work, but do not eat. When they displace labour, and render it disposable, they at the same time displace and render disposable the real wages, the food and clothing, which maintained it. The aggregate fund for the support of labour is not diminished, and therefore, unless the numbers to be maintained should increase, each individual, as soon as the free subsistence and free labour are readjusted to each other, will have the same command of the necessaries of life as before. But machines not only leave the aggregate fund for the maintenance of labour undiminished, they actually increase it. They are employed, because

they reduce productive cost; and whether such
reduction take place in agriculture, or in manufactures, it allows cultivation to extend over districts
which could not otherwise be tilled, and causes
additional funds for the maintenance of labour to
be created. When a machine is employed in
agriculture, the quantity of food and clothing expended in raising a given produce is reduced; and
when it is employed in manufactures, the value of
the clothing and implements expended in raising
a given produce is reduced; and therefore, in either
case, the plough is driven over regions into which
cultivation could not otherwise extend—the same
effect is produced as if increased natural fertility
had descended on the soil—the fund for the maintenance of labour is enlarged, and the same numbers will obtain higher wages, or additional numbers
will obtain employment.

Mr. Ricardo has stated an hypothetical case, in
which the employment of machinery might diminish the fund for the maintenance of labour, and
injure the working classes. The case is this.
Should any number of labourers, now employed in
producing the necessaries of life, be withdrawn
from that occupation, and employed in constructing
machines, the immediate consequence would be, a
diminution in the quantity of the necessaries of life;
and, as the diminished quantity would have to be
divided amongst the same number of persons as
before, a less quantity would fall to the share of each
individual, and real wages would be reduced. The
diminution of the funds for the maintenance of

labour, and the consequent fall of real wages, could only be temporary. As soon as the machines were completed, the labourers employed in constructing them would again become disposable for the production of necessaries, while the increased efficiency of industry, occasioned by a more extended application of mechanical power in aid of labour, would lead to extended tillage, and cause augmented supplies of food and raw material to be raised from soils which could not before remunerate the cultivator.

It is to be observed, that this hypothetical case, put by Mr. Ricardo, never occurs in practice. The labourers employed in agriculture, and in manufacturing necessary articles of clothing and furniture, are never withdrawn from these occupations for the purpose of constructing machines*. If, in any given year, the manufacture of machinery were to increase ten-fold, such increase would not occasion, even in that same year, any perceptible diminution in the supply of the necessaries of life.

The only case in which the employment of machinery can in practice diminish the funds for the maintenance of labour, is that in which the machinery is worked, not by mechanical, but by animal power. Should 100 labourers, employed in spade husbandry, consume 200 quarters of corn, and produce 220 quarters, the farmer, who advanced their consumption, would obtain 20 quarters as his profit. Now, let the plough be substituted

* See Senior's able Lectures on Wages.

for the spade, and horses for labourers, and then it
is possible that the profits of the farmer may be
increased, while the funds for the maintenance of
labour are diminished. For if 20 horses, consuming 40 quarters, can do the work of 50 men,
consuming 100 quarters, the farmer's whole expenditure will be reduced from 200 quarters to 140
quarters, and his return of 220 quarters to this
reduced expenditure, will leave 80 quarters instead
of 20 quarters, as his profit. But in this case, the
fund for the maintenance of labour would be
reduced to the whole extent of the consumption of
the horses. There will be 50 agricultural labourers
thrown out of employment; but there will not be,
as if the ploughs were worked by a non-food-con-
suming power, an equivalent supply of subsistence
set free to support them in other occupations.

It is to be remarked, however, that the injurious
effect of substituting horse power, for human labour,
would be gradually counteracted by the extended
tillage, rendered practicable by the diminution
effected in the cost of production. While the farmer employed in spade husbandry 100 men, consuming 200 quarters, he could not cultivate, with
the minimum profit of seven per cent., any land
yielding to this expenditure a less produce than 214
quarters. But when the substitution of ploughs
and horses reduces his expenditure from 200 to
140 quarters, he can immediately extend cultivation over inferior soils, yielding to this reduced
expenditure a produce of only 150 quarters; and
thus, by the extension of tillage, the funds for the

maintenance of labour would be again enlarged. In a country not exporting the raw produce of the soil, the permanent interest of the working classes must always be promoted by the substitution of a cheaper for a more expensive instrument of production. When cheaper instruments of production are employed, maximum or possible wages are raised, and unless the supply of labour increases with the increased power of extending cultivation over inferior soils, actual wages are made to approximate to their maximum.

The funds for the maintenance of labour receive their greatest possible increase, when, in the working of machines, horse power is superseded. In this case, human subsistence is augmented, not only by the extension of tillage rendered practicable by the reduction in the cost of production, but also by the whole quantity of produce which the horses formerly consumed. This most important augmentation in the supply of human subsistence has now commenced. Already in this country steam is superseding horses, and it is scarcely possible to measure the extent to which this supplanting process may be carried. In a few years draught horses may disappear from all the great lines of traffic throughout England; and it seems not improbable, that at no distant period the plough and the harrow will be moved by steam, as well as the carriage and the waggon. Upon the funds for the maintenance of labour, the substitution of steam for cattle will have the same effect as that which would be produced by doubling the fertility of the soil. There will be an unprecedented increase in the demand for labour; double the number of people may be employed at the same wages, or the same number at double wages.

From this examination of the results of machinery, it appears that all inventions for abridging labour, and diminishing the cost of production, with the exception of those in which cattle are employed as the moving power, augment the funds for the maintenance of labour, and have the effect of increasing both maximum and actual wages. It also appears, that the general good which results from the employment of new and improved machinery is accompanied by partial evil. While the public acquires additional wealth, the individuals who are supplanted in their accustomed occupations are reduced to poverty. Humanity and justice demand, that those who thus suffer for the public good should be relieved at the public expense. Whenever a new application of mechanical power throws a particular class of operatives out of employment, a national fund should be provided, to aid them in betaking themselves to other occupations. It is a disgrace to the Legislature and to the country, that the numerous body of hand-loom weavers should have been left so long in misery and destitution, and toiling to the death in hopeless competition with the power-loom. A comprehensive plan for their relief should be one of the earliest measures of the reformed Parliament.

CHAPTER III.

ON THE EFFECT OF COMBINATIONS FOR REDUCING WAGES.

In order to trace the effect of Combinations for Lowering Wages, let us suppose, in the first instance, that the farmers in an agricultural parish, in addition to their seed and implements, have each a fund of 200 quarters of corn for the maintenance of labour, which fund is advanced to 50 labourers. In this case, the real wages, estimated in corn, of each labourer, will be four quarters.

Let us now suppose, in the second instance, that all the farmers of the parish enter into a combination for reducing the wages of their workmen from four to three quarters; and that to this reduction the labourers are compelled to submit. The important question is, what would be the final effects of this combination?

It is obvious that the first effect must be a great increase in the profits of the farmers. All that the labourers lost, the farmers would gain.

It is equally obvious that the farmers could retain this advantage only so long as they agreed amongst themselves to employ their increased profits, not in adding to their capital, but in augmenting their unproductive expenditure. They could not employ additional capital without bidding against each other for additional hands, and thus breaking up the combination for the reduction of wages. The existence of the combination involves the necessity of devoting the whole of the increased profits, resulting from it, to immediate enjoyment.

This being the case, the reduction in agricultural wages gives to each farmer an additional revenue of 50 quarters of corn to be expended by his family in the decorations of dress and furniture. In the manufacturing towns, therefore, there will be an increased demand for those articles, while there will be a diminished demand for the wrought necessaries, used by the agricultural labourers whose wages are reduced. But the increase in the demand for manufactured luxuries, will be greater than the diminution in the demand for manufactured necessaries; because, the revenue which the agricultural labourers have lost was partly expended upon food, and partly upon manufactured goods; while the whole of the revenue which the farmers have gained, and which is equivalent to the whole which the labourers have lost, is expended upon manufactured luxuries. The result must, therefore, be a considerable increase in the demand for manufactured goods.

The increased demand for manufactured goods will create an increased demand for labour in the manufacturing towns; and in those towns, therefore, wages will advance. But if wages rise in the towns, while they fall in the country, a portion of the rural population will seek employment in the towns. A diminution in the supply of labour in one agricultural parish, threatening to contract cultivation, will therefore compel the farmers, notwithstanding their combination, to consent to an advance of wages.

But suppose that the combination for the reduction of wages extends to the towns, and that all master manufacturers agree together, to reduce the wages of their workmen, in the same proportion in which the farmers have reduced the wages of agricultural labour. The effects of this more extended combination it will be important to trace.

When, in the towns, the employers of labour have reduced wages by one-fourth, a considerable reduction will take place in the quantity and quality of the food consumed by the labouring classes in the towns. Hence, while the reduction of wages, and the consequent diminution in the consumption of food in the country districts, leave the farmers a greater quantity of agricultural produce to bring to market, the town demand for their produce will decline. One-fourth of the food and raw materials of necessaries, formerly consumed by the labouring class, will be unsaleable; one fourth of the land must be thrown out of cultivation; and one-fourth of the agricultural population must be transferred to the towns, there to fabricate the increased quantity of manufactured luxuries, for which the increase of profits creates a demand.

While this process is going on, there will be a great destruction of agricultural capital, and many farmers will be involved in distress and ruin. But we assume, for the sake of argument, that not-

withstanding the distress and ruin, through which
the class of farmers must pass in attaining their
object, they nevertheless adhere to the combination, and ultimately succeeded in effecting a
universal reduction of one-fourth in the rate of
wages. Let us endeavour to trace the consequences which would flow from this reduction.

The first effect of the universal reduction of
wages would be, an enormous rise in the rate of
profit. We can estimate, not indeed the exact,
but the proximate extent of this rise. It will be
determined by the average proportion which, before
they were reduced, wages bore to the whole advances of the capitalist. Thus, if wages, before
they were reduced, constituted one-half of the
capitalist's advances, their reduction by a fourth
would diminish his advances by an eighth ; and,
as his return would remain the same as before,
the extent of the increase of profits will immediately appear. For if, before the reduction of
wages, the farmers, or other capitalists, advanced 100 quarters as wages, and 100 quarters
for other outgoings, and obtained a reproduction
of 220 quarters, or a profit of 10 per cent., then
it is evident that when wages are reduced
from 100 to 75, the capitalist's reproduction of
220 to his reduced expenditure of 175, will
yield him a profit of 25 per cent. It is obvious,
that if, on the average, wages constituted more than
one-half of the whole advances, the rise of profits
would be greater ; while, if wages constituted less
than one-half the whole advances, the rise of profits

would be less. The principle is, that any given fall in the general rate of wages will cause a greater or less rise in the rate of profits, according as wages, on the average, form a greater or a less proportion of the capitalist's whole advances. For the purposes of our argument, it is a sufficient approximation to the actual state of things, to assume that wages form one-half of the capitalist's advances; and that, therefore, a general fall of wages, to the extent of one-fourth, will raise the rate of profit, if it had been 10 per cent. before the fall of wages, to 25 per cent.

Now the important practical questions for our consideration are, would it be possible to keep things in this state? Would it be practicable to perpetuate this forced depression of wages and rise of profits? A little careful inquiry will convince us that it would be quite impracticable, and that the final effect of the combination would be, not to raise profits at the expense of wages, but, on the contrary, to elevate wages at the expense of profits. Let us consider, in the first place, the circumstances which would render it impracticable to keep wages at the reduced level to which the combination of employers had forced them down, and then proceed to trace the reaction and recoil by which they would ascend, not merely to their former, but to a still higher level.

To keep wages at the low level to which, by the supposition, the combination has reduced them, it would be necessary that the following circumstances, each morally impossible, should concur :—

First.—It would be necessary that the whole of the employers of labour throughout the country, should expend the whole of their profits unproductively. No addition must be made to the aggregate amount of capital which they employ. The farmer must not extend his cultivation, nor the manufacturer increase his transactions. Children must not be put out to trade, but must continue to be dependent upon the profits realized by their parents, until their parents die off, and make place for them to carry on business on their own account. Should any of these events occur (and unless the principles and motives of human conduct were reversed, they would occur perpetually), the combination would be neutralized, the demand for labour would be increased, and wages would advance.

Secondly.—It would be necessary, not only that all farmers and master manufacturers, actually and directly employing labour, should abstain, as above, from increasing their capital, and extending their transactions; but also that all monied capitalists, bankers, merchants, traders, annuitants, civil and military functionaries, together with all landed proprietors throughout the country, should become parties to a combination for oppressing the labourer, and inflicting positive evil and grievous injury upon themselves. The whole of these classes must spend the whole of their incomes unproductively; or, if they make savings, must hoard them. Their accumulations, when made, they must neither employ productively themselves, nor lend out, to be employed productively by others. The reduction of wages has caused the rate of profit to rise to 25 per cent., and the throwing out of one-fourth of the land which supplied the labouring classes with food and the raw materials of manufactured necessaries, by limiting the necessary extent of tillage to soils of a superior quality, must have occasioned a still further increase of profits, and have raised them to 30, perhaps to 35 per cent. The natural effect of a high rate of profit is to raise the rate of interest also. If 30, or even 25 per cent. could be made by the employment of borrowed capital, individuals destitute of capital themselves, but having the skill, industry, and integrity which command credit, might be willing to give 15 or 20 per cent. for the use of money. But if money be lent to be employed productively, the combination cannot be maintained. In order to maintain it, it is necessary that persons having money at command should hoard it in strong boxes, or bury it under ground, rather than lend it at 15 or 20 per cent. Again, the combination for the reduction of wages has thrown out of cultivation one-fourth of the land which formerly supplied the labouring population with food and the materials of wrought necessaries, and has therefore occasioned a total loss of rent upon all the lands thrown out, and a considerable fall of rents upon all the better soils still remaining under tillage. In order to maintain the combination, it is further necessary that the landed proprietors should join in the league for reducing and destroying the value of their own property. They must not lend their money, or their credit, at an interest of 15 or 20 per cent. to industrious and honest tenants, who would cultivate the lands which had been thrown out, and occasion a recovery of rents; because, should they advance their money, or their credit, for such a purpose, the funds for the maintenance of labour would be increased, wages would rise, and the effect of the combination would be destroyed.

Thirdly.—It would be necessary, in order to maintain the combination, that the influx of foreign capital should be prohibited. Though all the farmers and master manufacturers throughout the country should join in the conspiracy for the reduction of wages; and though monied capitalists, and merchants, and bankers, and annuitants, and public functionaries, and landed proprietors, should enter into a solemn league and covenant, to lend neither money, nor credit, to any one desirous of engaging in the work of production, yet the combination would be inoperative and abortive if the importation of foreign capital were permitted. The rate of profit has a tendency to preserve a certain level, not only throughout the several districts of the same country, but also throughout the several countries of the commercial world. Should the depression of wages, and the throwing out of inferior land, raise the rate of profit, in England, in any considerable degree above the level it had ordinarily preserved, in relation to the rates of profit in Holland and in France, the disengaged and floating capital of these countries would flow into England, and there seek productive investment. The combination would therefore be ineffectual, unless the conspirators against wages could secure the co-operation of the Legislature, and obtain an Act of Parliament prohibiting the importation of food and of raw materials, and all the ingredients of directly productive capital, which constitute the fund for the maintenance of labour.

After this enumeration of the circumstances which must concur, in order to give effect to a combination for the reduction of wages, it would be superfluous to go into any argument or illustration to show that the maintenance of such a combination would be utterly impracticable. It is only necessary to trace out the process by which, were it possible, which it clearly is not, to give such a combination a brief and partial existence, it would necessarily counterwork itself, and ultimately tend, not to depress, but to elevate wages.

We have seen that the minimum below which wages cannot permanently fall, consists of that quantity of the necessaries of life which is requisite to keep up the labouring population ; and we have seen, that this quantity of necessaries is not a fixed immutable quantity, but varies under different climates, and under the influence of different habits of living. It is self-evident, that should wages be at their *physical* minimum, as determined by climate, a combination depressing them below this point would cut off a portion of the population ; that it would diminish the supply of labour in relation to the demand; and that its ultimate effect would be, not to depress but to elevate wages. A moment's consideration will render it apparent, that should wages be at the *moral* minimum, as determined by habits of living, a combination for depressing them, if for a time successful, would be followed by similar results.

Custom is a second nature, and things not originally necessary to healthful existence become so from habit. Though the Irish peasantry, living upon potatoes and butter-milk, are not subjected to greater mortality than their neighbours, yet were the labouring classes in England, brought up upon the more substantial diet of bread and cheese, and butchers' meat, reduced to the less nutritious food which use has rendered not unhealthful in Ireland, debility and disease would rapidly thin their ranks. A higher rate of mortality among the labouring classes would speedily follow the establishment of a combination for reducing wages. Where there were numerous families they would be thinned by death ; the delicate and infirm would sink prematurely to the grave ; and while more died, fewer would be born. The cautious and the prudent, and those who were attached to the former superior scale of comfort, would abstain from marriage, and from encumbering themselves with families; and thus, by rendering deaths more numerous and births less frequent, an effectual combination for the reduction of wages, however brief its existence, would, for a whole generation, reduce the supply of labour in relation to the demand. Nothing could now prevent the recoil of wages. An effective combination for the reduction of wages would bear within it the principle of almost immediate self-destruction ; and, after a brief existence, would leave wages at a higher level than that from which they had fallen. For, the instant the combination should be broken up, increased capital accumulated at home, or imported from abroad, would be employed in cultivating the land which had been abandoned, and in supplying the renewed consumption of the necessaries of life. Thus there would be an increased demand for labour, acting upon a diminished supply. The supply of labour, in relation both to land and capital, would be less than before, and, therefore, upon the principles already explained, both maximum and actual wages would be higher than before.

From all that has been said, it must be apparent, that an effectual combination for the reduction of wages can never by possibility exist. In the first place, such a combination could not be established ; and, in the second place, if it could be established, it could not be maintained. If

not immediately broken up, by productive advances, made from income, or by the importation
of capital from abroad, it would speedily perish
by self-destruction; and its evil influence, after
having for a time afflicted the labouring classes,
would recoil upon the insane conspirators, lowering, instead of raising, the rate of profit, and
elevating, instead of depressing, wages.

CHAPTER IV.

ON THE EFFECT OF COMBINATIONS FOR RAISING WAGES.

In a country not depending upon foreign markets, Combinations may raise Wages to their maximum, provided the supply of labour do not increase.

The labouring classes form the great majority of every community, and, as has been already observed, a country must be considered as happy or miserable, in proportion as those classes are abundantly or scantily supplied with the necessaries and comforts of life. From this principle it necessarily follows, that combinations for lowering wages, could they be effectual, must be regarded as conspiracies for increasing human misery; and that combinations for raising wages, could they be effectual, must be approved as associations for the promotion of human happiness. In the whole compass of economical science, the most important practical question is this, namely, can combinations, amongst the labouring classes, effect a permanent increase of wages?

It is evident, that if wages were already at their maximum, a combination which should have the immediate effect of raising wages, must speedily terminate in reducing them. When wages are at their maximum, profits are at their minimum. But when profits are at their minimum, an increase of wages must check production, diminish the fund for the maintenance of labour, and leave for each labourer a less quantity of the comforts and necessaries of life.

Supposing, as in our former cases, that the lowest rate of profit, for the sake of which the capitalist will continue the work of production, is seven per cent., then, should the farmer, advancing 100 quarters of corn for seed, and 100 quarters for the wages of 25 men, cultivate a tract of land yielding 214 quarters, profits would be at their minimum, and wages at their maximum. Under those circumstances, if the 25 labourers were to combine together, and refuse to work, unless their wages were raised from 100 to 115 quarters, it is evident that all profit would be absorbed, that the tract of land must be abandoned, and that the 25 labourers, instead of continuing to receive the increased wages which they demanded from the farmer, would, at no distant period, be thrown out of work.

Now, suppose that profits, instead of being at the minimum of seven per cent., were 10 per cent. In this case, wages might rise so as to reduce profits by three per cent., before the last quality of land under tillage would be thrown out of cultivation. Our 25 labourers might therefore combine, until each received as his wages four quarters, and the fraction of a quarter, instead of four quarters. But should this immediate improvement in their condition, by diminishing deaths, or increasing births, cause their numbers to increase from 25 to 27, the ultimate result would be, not an advance, but a decline of wages. When the farmer, cultivating a tract of land yielding 220 quarters, advanced 100 quarters as seed, and 100 quarters as wages to 25 labourers, he realised a profit of ten quarters, which is three per cent. above the assumed minimum. But if he advances 100 quarters as seed, and four quarters each to 27 labourers, his advances will be 208 quarters, and will yield a profit less than the minimum of seven per cent. He will, therefore, either reduce the wages of his 27 labourers below the original rate of four quarters a man, or else abandon his farm, and throw them out of employment.

In a country growing its own supplies of raw produce, not exporting manufactured goods, and therefore not exposed to foreign competition, a combination for raising wages can be maintained only when accompanied by an auxiliary combination amongst the labouring classes, for preventing the increase of their numbers. Let us proceed to consider the effect of a combination for raising wages in a country which, importing raw materials, and exporting manufactured goods, is exposed to foreign competition. This is the practical, and, to the operatives of England, the vitally important branch of the subject.

In a country depending upon foreign markets,
Combinations for raising Wages beyond the
limit determined by foreign competition, ulti-
mately occasion, not an advance, but a reduction
of Wages.

As before we will assume, for the sake of illustration, that the actual rates of profit in England and
in France are ten per cent., and that, in both
countries, the minimum rate of profit, without which
the capitalist will not continue production, is seven
per cent. Under these circumstances, let us suppose
that the operatives in England combine, and obtain
such an increase of wages as will reduce the profits
of their masters to the minimum of seven per cent.
In this case the English manufacturer cannot permanently reduce the price of his goods in the foreign
market, because, if he did, he could not realise
minimum profits. But the French manufacturer
can afford to undersell the British manufacturer
in the foreign market, by one, two, or three per
cent., and still realise his minimum profit of seven
per cent. ; and, therefore, the necessary effect of the
combination will be, to cause the manufacturers of
France to drive the manufacturers of England out
of the foreign market.

Writers upon commercial policy, whose opinions
are entitled to great respect, have contended that a
rise of wages has no influence upon foreign trade.
They maintain, that a rise of wages is accompanied
by a corresponding fall of profits, and does not
therefore raise prices ; and they further affirm,

that a fall in the rate of profit does not subject the country in which it takes place, to be undersold in the foreign market, by other countries in which profits are. higher*. The reason advanced for the doctrine, that high wages and low profits do not subject a country to any disadvantage in the foreign market is this—Should a lower rate of wages render the cost of production in France three per cent. less than in England, and should the rate of profit be three per cent. higher in France than in England, the French producers might sell their goods in any foreign market, three per cent. lower than the English producers could sell similar goods, by consenting, like the English producers, to accept a profit of seven per cent. But it is contended that, under these circumstances, the French producers would not consent to mauufacture for the foreign market, at a profit of seven per cent., for the obvious reason, that they could make 10 per cent. upon their capital in any occupation.

This argument, when stated in general terms, appears, at first sight, satisfactory; but, when considered strictly and analytically, it will be seen to be wholly fallacious. The subject is so very important, that it requires a detailed examination.

Let us suppose that an English and a French manufacturer have each invested 50,000*l.* in buildings and machinery, and that they each

* M‘Culloch.

expend, in a year, 50,000*l.* in materials and wages. Let us also suppose that, in consequence of lower wages in France, the French manufacturer is able to employ more labourers, and to use more material than the English, and therefore fabricates, by six per cent. upon his floating capital, a greater quantity of goods. The goods being similar in kind, and in quality, the prices obtained for them in the foreign market will be in proportion to their quantities, and the French manufacturer will sell his goods for a greater sum, by six per cent. upon his floating capital of 50,000*l.*, than the English. If the English goods sold for 57,000*l.*, the French, being greater in quantity in the proportion stated, would sell for 60,000*l.* Under these circumstances, would it be the interest of the French manufacturer to sell his greater quantity of goods for the same sum that the English manufacturer sold the less quantity, and thus secure a superiority in the foreign market ?

When the Englishman sells his goods for 57,000*l.*, he replaces his floating capital, and obtains a profit of seven per cent., both upon his floating and upon his fixed capital; and when the Frenchman sells his goods for 60,000*l.*, he replaces his advance for wages and materials, and realizes a profit of ten per cent. upon his whole capital. Now, if the Frenchman would sell his greater quantity of goods for the same sum for which the Englishman sells the less quantity, and would be satisfied for a short time with seven per cent. upon his original capital of 100,000*l*., he might undersell the English manufacturer, and drive his goods out of the foreign market. The French manufacturer might now sell double his former quantity of goods. He might advance an additional 50,000*l*. in wages and materials, and sell the additional quantity of goods for an additional sum of 57,000*l*.; and, should no additional outlay be requisite for buildings and machines, this would yield him, on his second portion of floating capital, a profit, not of seven, but of fourteen per cent. It is self-evident, therefore, that if a greater quantity of materials can be worked up without an additional outlay for fixed capital, it will be the interest of the French manufacturer to take less than the average rate of profit in France upon the first portion of his advances, in order to gain more than this average rate upon the additional portions of floating capital, which he can employ by underselling the English manufacturer, and beating him out of the foreign market.

It must be apparent, that the force of this argument depends upon the fact, whether, in manufacturing industry, additional floating capital can be employed without a proportionate addition of fixed capital. Now with respect to the matter of fact there can be no doubt. The market is occasionally under-stocked, and occasionally overstocked, with manufactured goods. When the supply of such goods is deficient their production is increased;

and when their supply is in excess, their production is diminished. But when the production of manufactured goods diminishes, the fixed capital of the manufacturer ceases to be fully employed. It is self-evident, therefore, that, amid the ebbings and flowings of the market, and the alternate contractions and expansions of demand, occasions will constantly recur, in which the manufacturer may employ additional floating capital, without employing additional fixed capital. It admits of the strictest demonstration, that if additional quantities of raw material can be worked up without incurring an additional expense for buildings and machinery, the manufacturers of the country in which the rate of profit is comparatively high, will have an interest in lowering their prices in the foreign market, so as to beat out the fabrics of the country in which the rate of profit is comparatively low.

The French and English manufacturers invest, each, 50,000*l*. in buildings and machines ; and, when their fixed capital is in full action, each can employ a floating capital of 50,000*l*. in wages and raw materials. The Frenchman, paying less for labour, is able to work up more material, and produces a quantity of goods greater to the extent of six per cent. upon his floating capital of 50,000*l*. than the quantity produced by the Englishman. The goods of each being similar in kind and quality, if those of the Englishman sell for 57,000*l*. those of the Frenchman will sell for 60,000*l*. Now it is self-evident, that, under these circumstances, it would not be the interest of the French manufacturer to undersell the English, and drive him from the foreign market. For his machinery being fully employed, he cannot advance additional floating capital for wages and materials, without making a proportional addition to his fixed capital; and he cannot realize 10 per cent., the customary rate of profit in France, upon his advances, unless the goods produced by a fixed capital of 50,000*l.*, and a floating capital of 50,000*l.*, continue to sell in the foreign market for 60,000*l.* He cannot, therefore, undersell the English manufacturer without employing additional capital in the foreign trade, at a less rate of profit than that which he might obtain in other occupations.

Very different would be the result, should a revulsion of trade check production, and prevent the fixed capital invested in manufactures from being fully employed. Let us suppose that the quantity of goods on hand is so much in excess, that our manufacturers are obliged to diminish the supply, and, instead of employing a floating capital of 50,000*l.* each, can employ floating capital of only 25,000*l.* each. In this case, the factories will work only half time; only half the quantity of goods will be produced, and, prices remaining the same*, the Frenchman's goods, instead of selling for 60,000*l.*

---

* Under the circumstances, prices would fall; but this, instead of weakening the case as now put, would render it still stronger.

will sell for only 30,000*l.* This will replace his floating capital of 25,000*l.* with a surplus of 5000*l.*, which will amount to a profit of six and two-thirds per cent. upon his whole capital of 75,000*l.* Under these circumstances, it will be the decided interest of the French manufacturer to lower his prices, and drive the English manufacturer out of the foreign market. By doing so, he will be able to employ an additional floating capital of 25,000*l.*, without incurring an additional expense for fixed capital; and may produce an additional quantity of goods, greater by three per cent. than the quantity which the English manufacturer sold for 28,500*l.* Should he sell his greater quantity, for the same sum of 28,500*l.*, for which the English manufacturer sold his less quantity, he will drive the English manufacturer out of the foreign market, and obtain a return of 28,500*l.* for an advance of 25,000*l.* This will be a profit of 14 per cent. upon the additional floating capital employed. Now, by the supposition, the general rate of profit in France is only 10 per cent. Instead of obtaining less, the French manufacturer will gain much more than the customary rate of profit, by employing all the floating capital he can command, in fabricating more goods at lower prices, and thereby expelling competitors from the foreign market.

Thus we see that the argument, so confidently advanced in support of the doctrine, that a rise of wages has no injurious effect upon foreign trade, is altogether erroneous, and involves the fallacy, unfortunately too prevalent amongst economical writers, of confounding distinctions by hasty generalizations, and of attributing to different things the same common properties, because we class them under the same common name.

The buildings and machines of the manufacturer, as well as the money with which he pays his wages, and purchases his raw materials, are classed under the general denomination of capital; and those who, in their proneness for general reasoning, forget that science is analysis, fall into the error of conceiving, that because capital, consisting of money, may pass from employment to employment, in order to obtain the customary rate of profit, capital, consisting of buildings and machinery, may be equally locomotive. The reasoning in support of the position, that high comparative wages, and low comparative profits, are not injurious to foreign trade, and do not involve the danger of foreign competition, would be perfectly correct, provided fixed capital were not fixed. If money sunk in buildings and machinery could be made to realize the same customary rate of profit when the machinery is not employed, as when it is employed, then, indeed, the manufacturers in a country in which profits were comparatively high, would have no inducement to undersell the manufacturer of a country in which the customary rate of profits were low; because, in this case, the high comparative rate of profit might, at all times, be obtained upon the whole capital, fixed as well as floating, which the manufacturers of the high-profit-country employed. But so long as buildings and machinery, when not in work, exist as dead stock, realizing no profit at all, so long will it be the interest of producers to employ, at the customary rate of profit, as much of their floating capital as possible, without reference to the consideration whether, by so employing it, they realize the customary profit upon their fixed capital also. This is a consideration which will always determine whether new and additional buildings and machines shall be erected; but when once they are erected, it will be the decided interest of the manufacturer to keep them in full work, provided he can thereby secure the customary profit upon the floating capital employed in paying wages, and in purchasing raw materials. Hence, when the foreign market is overstocked, it will be the interest of the manufacturer of the high-profit-country to continue to supply it at prices greatly below those ordinary prices which gave the customary return upon his whole capital, fixed and floating. This customary profit on his whole capital was necessary to induce him to *commence* business, but is not necessary to induce him to *continue* it. To secure this, it is sufficient that he obtains the customary profit upon that portion of his capital which he can transfer without loss to other occupations.

An objection may here be urged. It may be contended, that the argument cuts both ways, and is as applicable to the manufacturers of the low-profit, as to the manufacturers of the high-profit-country. If it be the interest of the latter to continue to supply the foreign market, at prices so reduced as to leave the customary rate of profit only on the moveable portion of their capital, it must be the interest of the former to do so likewise. But if the manufacturers of the low-profit-country found it their interest to continue to supply the foreign market at a reduction of prices which left them customary profits on their floating capital only, the manufacturers of the high-profit-country could not undersell them without a diminution of their customary rate of profit upon that portion of their capital which they could transfer to more advantageous occupations. It follows, therefore, that a comparatively low rate of profit cannot have the effect of contracting the extent of foreign trade.

This objection proceeds upon the assumption, that prices in the foreign market never fall below that point at which the manufacturer obtains his customary rate of profit upon that portion of his capital which can be transferred without loss to other occupations; and, were this assumption conformable to fact, the objection would be valid and conclusive. But the assumption is contrary to fact. Frequent is the fall of prices below the point supposed. Revulsions occasionally occur, during which the manufacturer scarcely obtains a return sufficient to replace the floating capital he advances. Nay, in the vibrations of the market, the depression of trade will sometimes be so great that the manufacturer cannot, at existing prices, replace his floating capital, and that he continues to advance wages and materials at a positive loss, because he cannot, without incurring a greater loss, abandon his buildings and machinery; or because he is able to keep his goods on hand until the glut is removed, and prices have recovered. Now, on all such occasions, the manufacturers of the high-profit-country will have a decided advantage over those of the low-profit-country, and will drive them out of the foreign market. Let us exemplify this process by a reference to our former case.

A French manufacturer advances a floating capital of 50,000*l.*, and produces 10,300 bales of goods; an English manufacturer also advances a floating capital of 50,000*l.*, but, as from the higher rate of wages which he pays, can employ fewer hands, and purchase less material, he produces only 10,000 bales. Under these circumstances, let us suppose that the prices of the foreign market fall so low, that the English 10,000 bales sell there for no more than 50,000*l.*, while the French 10,300 bales, of the same kind and quality, sell for a greater sum in proportion to their greater quantity, or for 51,500*l.* In this case the English manufacturer just saves himself, while the French manufacturer realizes a profit of three per cent. upon his floating capital.

Let us now suppose that the prices in the foreign market continue to decline, until the Frenchman's

10,300 bales, produced by a floating capital of 50,000*l.*, sell for no more than 50,000*l.* and the Englishman's bales, produced by the same expenditure, sell for a less sum in proportion to their less quantity. In this case the Frenchman will just save himself, while the Englishman will incur a positive loss.

Thus it is self-evident, that in all revulsions of foreign trade there will be, in the country in which profits are comparatively low, a much heavier loss, and a much greater destruction of capital, than in countries in which profits are comparatively high. Should the difference in the rates of profit be considerable, the high-profit-country may continue to realize moderate gains under a revulsion of foreign trade, and depression of the markets, which spread bankruptcy and ruin throughout the manufacturing districts of the low-profit-country.

One other consideration remains, and it is a most important one. Floating capital has a constant tendency to transfer itself from countries in which profits are low to those in which they are high. Love of country, the inconvenience of conforming to foreign manners, and the difficulty of acquiring foreign languages, may, to a certain extent, counteract this tendency; but, notwithstanding these barriers to a perfect equalization, this tendency of profits, throughout the commercial countries of the civilized world, to gravitate towards a common level, will prevent capital from resting on those places where the cost of production has been unduly elevated. We may lay it down as a principle established by a complete induction from experience, that manufacturing industry will establish, and extend itself, in those countries in which manufacturing capital obtains a high comparative reward ; and will partly be driven, and partly retire of its own accord, from those districts in which manufacturing profits are comparatively low.

From these illustrations, which the vital importance of the subject has led us thus to extend into demonstrative details, we can distinctly trace the ultimate effect, upon the working classes, of combinations for raising wages, in a country which exports manufactured goods. In such country the price of manufactured goods in the foreign market cannot exceed the price at which they can be supplied by the foreign producer. Now, when the price of goods is thus fixed, every increase of wages, other things remaining the same, must increase the cost of production upon the domestic producer, and lower the rate of his profit ; and this reduction of profit must expose him to the successful competition of those foreign manufacturing countries, in which a corresponding increase of wages has not occasioned a similar fall in the rate of profit. Upon every revulsion of trade, and stagnation of the market, this fall of profits will cause the domestic producer to be undersold in the foreign market ; will compel him to contract, or to discontinue his operations, and to throw his labourers partially, or wholly, out of employment. The labourers, thus thrown out, will not be able to obtain other employment at the same rate of wages as before ; because, as a less quantity of manufactured goods can be exported, a less quantity of raw material and of food can be imported, and the general fund for the maintenance of labour will be diminished. Now, if the whole of the fund for the maintenance of labour, the whole quantity of food and material, be diminished, it is self-evident, that the number of labourers remaining the same, each individual must receive less real wages than before. It thus appears, by proof amounting to strictly mathematical demonstration, that in a country exporting manufactured goods, an effectual combination for increasing wages, which should have the effect of lowering the rate of profit below the rate obtained in other manufacturing countries, must ultimately terminate, not in an advance, but in a reduction of wages.

In a country possessing superiority in manufacturing for the foreign markets, Wages may be raised within the limits of such superiority.

By the terms in which the important principle demonstrated in the preceding section is stated, it will be apparent, that it is liable, in practice, to two exceptions. It is by increasing the cost of production, and by rendering profits comparatively low, that successful combinations for raising wages contract the field of industry, and limit foreign trade, and thus ultimately terminate in throwing labour out of employment, and in rendering wages lower than before. It follows, that, were they formed under circumstances which should prevent an increase in the cost of production, and a relative fall in the rate of profit, such combinations, instead of creating this injurious reaction, might permanently secure, to the labouring classes, a larger share of the necessaries and comforts of life. Here, then, a very important practical question arises, namely, what accompanying circumstances will prevent a rise of wages from increasing the cost of production, and from reducing the rate of profit below the rates obtained in other countries? Let us inquire.

Should a labourer, when he demands, and obtains, an advance of wages, execute an additional quantity of work proportional to this advance, it is evident that no increase of productive cost, no decline in the rate of profit, could be thereby occasioned. If the farmer and the manufacturer paid more for labour, they would cultivate and manufacture more. The increase in their returns being in the same proportion as the increase in their advances, the cost of production, and the rate of profit, would remain the same. A greater quantity of necessaries and comforts would be produced, the fund for the maintenance of labour would be increased; and this increased fund, divided amongst the same number of individuals, would give an increased quantity of necessaries to each. It is obvious, nay, it is self-evident, that should a combination for raising wages be accompanied by an ancillary combination for increasing the hours of labour, and the quantity of work, in the same proportion in which wages might be increased, it would give to the labouring classes an increased supply of the comforts and necessaries of life. It might be difficult, it might be impracticable, to establish these co-operating combinations ; but, were they once fairly established, no injurious reaction, or recoil, could be occasioned, and wages would be permanently increased.

There is another limitation of the principle, that, in a country exporting manufactured goods, and importing food and raw materials, the ultimate effect of combinations for raising wages is, to reduce them below the previous level. In such a country the manner in which a compulsory elevation, occasions a permanent depression of wages, is, by reducing the rates of profit below the rates obtained in other manufacturing countries, and thus giving to such countries a superiority in the foreign market. Now, should the particular country in which the compulsory rise of wages took place, possess an advantage over other manufacturing countries, in supplying the articles demanded in the foreign market, this particular country might pay high comparative wages, and yet retain its superiority with respect to foreign trade, provided the disadvantage created by the high wages, were less than the advantage arising from other causes. For example, if, in fabricating a given quantity of cloth, the English manufacturer expends 100*l.* in fuel and machinery, 100*l.* in materials, and 100*l.* in wages ; while the French manufacturer expends 150*l.* in fuel and machinery, 100*l.* in material, and 100*l.* in wages ; then it is evident, that a combination might raise wages in England from 100*l.* to 140*l.*, and yet leave to England the power of underselling France in the foreign market. The disadvantage arising from the high price of labour in England, would be more than counterbalanced by the advantage created by the low price of fuel and machinery. After the rise of wages, the whole cost of producing the cloth in England will be 340*l.*, while in France it will be 350*l.* ; and the French manufacturer will still be unable to compete with the English in the foreign market. Nor would such a rise in the reward of labour be injurious to the employers of labour.

In a country which can manufacture for the foreign market at a less cost than others, a compulsory rise of wages, provided it did not go the length of equalizing productive cost, would not have the effect of reducing manufacturing profits. Under such circumstances, the price of manufactured goods would rise in the foreign market, and it would be the foreign consumer, and not the home capitalist, who would pay the advance of wages obtained by the operative class. The great value and importance of this fact will justify us in again resorting to the details of an illustrative example.

If, in England and in France, the cost of production were equal, and the ordinary rate of profit 10 per cent., then should the English and the French manufacturer expend each 100*l.* in fabricating and conveying a given quantity of cloth for the foreign market, in that market this quantity of cloth would sell for 110*l.* Now, suppose that, in England, the discovery of cheaper fuel, or an improved machine, enables the manufacturer to fabricate and convey this quantity of cloth for 90*l.*, instead of for 100*l* ; then, while it continues to sell in the foreign market for 110*l.*, he will realize a profit of 22 per cent. But this high rate of profit would attract capital to the business of fabricating cloth, until the increasing supply of the article so reduced its price, as to leave the producer no more than the ordinary profit of 10 per cent. The quantity of cloth which had sold for 110*l.*, when its productive cost was 100*l.*, will sell for no more than 99*l.*, when its cost is reduced to 90*l.* The French manufacturer would be driven out of the foreign market : but though the English manufacturer would obtain the exclusive supplying of that market, and would consequently be able to sell a much larger quantity of goods than before, yet, *domestic competition* would effectually prevent him from realizing a higher rate of profit than before.

Let us now suppose, that, after these effects have been produced, the operatives in England combine, and obtain an advance of wages, which raises the cost of fabricating the given quantity of cloth, from 90 to 98, while this quantity of cloth continues to sell in the foreign market for no more than 99. This advance of wages will reduce the manufacturer's profit from 10 to little more than one per cent. But capital would gradually be withdrawn from an occupation yielding so slender a return; and, even if not withdrawn from the actual fabrication of cloth, the more wealthy manufacturers would keep their goods on hand, until the diminished supply in the foreign market elevated prices, and enabled them to realize ordinary profits. The quantity of cloth which, before the rise of wages, and the consequent increased cost of production, had sold for 99*l.*, will now sell for 108*l.* in the foreign market. This rise in the price of British goods will not, however, deprive the British manufacturer of the exclusive supply of the foreign market; for, by this supposition, he is still able to undersell the French manufacturer, by nearly two per cent. But, if the British manufacturer realizes the same rate of profit as before, and retains, as before, the exclusive supply of the foreign market, it is evident, that the advance of wages obtained by the operative, must be paid by the foreign consumer, in the increased price of cloth.

Thus it appears, upon the fullest evidence, that in a country possessing a superiority over other manufacturing countries, in producing goods

for the foreign market, the rate of wages may
be increased above the rates obtained in other
countries to nearly the whole extent of such superiority, without reducing the rate of profit, or
exposing the manufacturer to foreign competition.
But it will also appear, upon evidence equally
conclusive, that this higher scale of wages cannot
be maintained, if the operatives increase their
numbers beyond the demand for labour. If, in any
neighbourhood, one thousand hands are required
to fabricate the goods demanded in the foreign
market, and if the hands increase from one
thousand to eleven hundred, no possible combination
amongst the operatives can avert a fall of wages.
We have seen, that all that it is possible for the
most perfect combination to perform is, to increase
the rate of wages to nearly the whole extent of
whatever superiority the country may possess, in
supplying goods for the foreign market. When
a rise of wages to this extent has been obtained
for that number of labourers which may be required to fabricate the quantity of goods demanded
in the foreign market, the price of labour cannot
be further increased, without losing the foreign
market. But if a combination so limited the
hours of labour, that it required eleven hundred
to do the work formerly done by a thousand, and if
each of the eleven hundred should receive the same
wages formerly received by each of the thousand,
the price of labour and the cost of production
would be increased, the foreign market would be

lost, and the whole of the labourers which supplied
it would be thrown out of employment. If the
combination should limit the hours of labour, the
wages of each labourer must be reduced, in proportion to the diminution in the work he performed; and should the combination, without
reducing the hours of labour, limit the number
of hands who should offer themselves for employment, those who were employed would have
to maintain those who were unemployed, which
would be the same thing in effect, as a reduction
of wages. To retain possession of the foreign
market, and at the same time to increase the price
of a given quantity of work, beyond the proportion
of the superiority possessed in supplying the
foreign market, is manifestly impossible. But if the
price of a given quantity of work cannot be increased, while the hands employed in performing it
are increased, it is self-evident that the wages of
each individual must be reduced. In a country possessing superiority in supplying goods for the
foreign market, a combination, could it be formed
and maintained, might effect an advance of wages,
within the limits of that superiority, provided the
number of hands seeking for employment, did not
increase in a greater proportion than the quantity
of work to be performed.

The Corn Laws deprive the operatives of England of the high comparative Wages due to the superiority which England possesses in manufacturing for the foreign market.

The principles which have been established in the preceding section are liable to exception and limitation, in their application to the actual circumstances of this country. In England, the operatives execute in a given time, say a week or a month, a much greater quantity of work than the operatives of the continent; and, in England, coal, and iron, canals, railroads, coasts, harbours, and geographical position, give to the manufacturer a most decided superiority in supplying the foreign market with manufactured goods. Yet, notwithstanding all these peculiar advantages which he possesses, the English manufacturer is so nearly undersold by the foreigner, that any material advance in the real wages of the operative classes, would disable him from encountering the competition to which he is exposed; and, if rendered compulsory, either by an act of the Legislature, or by combination among the working people, would destroy manufacturing profits, and transfer the seats of manufacturing industry to other countries.

These facts, apparently so irreconcilable, are fully established by the evidence given before successive parliamentary committees. The fact, that the operatives in England execute, in a given

time, a much greater quantity of work than the
operatives of the continent, is proved by the witnesses examined by the Committee on Artisans
and Machinery, which sat in the session of 1824.
Many of these witnesses were English manufacturers, who had worked in France. They agree
as to the comparative indolence of the French
labourer, even during his hours of employment.
One of the witnesses, Adam Young, had been two
years in one of the best manufactories of Alsace*.
He is asked, " Did you find the spinners there, as
" industrious as the spinners in England ? " and
replies, " No ; a spinner in England will do twice
" as much as a Frenchman ; they get up at four
" in the morning, and work till ten at night ; but
" our spinners will do as much in six hours as
" they will do in ten."

" Had you any Frenchmen employed under
" you ?"—" Yes, eight."

" Supposing you had eight English corders
" under you, how much more work could you have
" done ? "—" With one Englishman I could have
" done more work than I did with those eight
" Frenchmen. It cannot be called work they do ;
" it is only looking at it, and wishing it done."

Upon general principles, this great superiority
in the efficacy of British labour, aided, as it is,
by better machinery, cheaper fuel, and cheaper
carriage, should give an extensive margin, enabling

* SENIOR's Lectures on Wages.

the operatives of England to obtain a considerable increase of wages above those of their continental brethren, without depriving the British manufacturer of his superiority in the foreign market, or exposing him to the danger of foreign competition. But we find, by the evidence given before the Committee of the Session of 1833, that the British manufacturer is already standing upon that extreme and dangerous verge, beyond which his foreign rival can encounter him upon equal terms; and that an increase of wages, relatively to the wages obtained upon the continent, would deprive him of his footing in the foreign market. What then is the counteracting circumstance which takes from the operative classes of England the power of obtaining an increase of wages, within the limits of the great superiority in the efficacy of their labour arising from the extraordinary advantages, natural and acquired, which they possess? This counteracting circumstance is the high price of food; and the cause of the high price of food, is the existing Corn Laws. A very brief illustration will be sufficient to demonstrate, that while the price of corn in England remains nearly twice as high as upon the continent, it is morally impossible for the English operative to obtain, either an increase of wages, or a diminution in the hours of his toil.

Let the expense of manufacturing a given quantity of cloth in England and in France be as stated in the following cases :

CASE I.—ENGLAND.

Wages of 200 men, at 4 quarters of corn per man, 800 quarters, at 40*s*. per quarter - - -	£. 1600
Raw materials - - -	400
Fuel, wear and tear of machinery -	950
Carriage - - -	50
Total cost to English manufacturer	£. 3000

CASE II.—FRANCE.

Wages of 300 men, at 2 quarters per man, 600 quarters, at 40*s*. per quarter - - - - -	£.1200
Raw materials - - -	400
Fuel, wear and tear of machinery -	1350
Carriage - - -	80
Total cost to French manufacturer	£. 3030

In these cases, the price of provisions is assumed to be equal; but as 200 English operatives work up as much material as 300 French, and as the expense of machinery, and fuel, and carriage, which is only 1000*l*. in England, is 1430*l*. in France, the

English manufacturer can afford to undersell the French manufacturer in the foreign market by one per cent., though in England the real rate of wages is 100 per cent. higher than in France.

Now let us suppose, that while all other things remain the same, the first necessaries of life become 100 per cent. dearer in England than in France; the price of a quarter of corn rising from 40s. to 80s. in the former country, and remaining at 40s. in the latter. In this case the English manufacturer cannot retain his former superiority in the foreign market, without making a deduction of 50 per cent., or one half in the corn-wages of his workmen. Thus,

CASE III.—ENGLAND.

Wages of 200 men, at 2 quarters of
   corn per man, 400 quarters, at
   80s. per quarter   -   -   -   £. 1600
Raw materials   -   -   -   400
Fuel and machinery   -   -   950
Carriage   -   -   -   50

   Cost to English manufacturer   £.3000

   Cost to French manufacturer
      as in Case II.   -   -   £. 3030

Under these circumstances, if our 200 English labourers were to combine, and refuse to work until they obtained 425 quarters, this trifling difference of the eighth part of a quarter of corn in the real wages of each individual, would drive the manufacturer from the foreign market, and would throw out of employment all those who depended upon the foreign trade for their subsistence. For if the English manufacturer, when corn was at 80*s*., advanced to his 200 labourers 425 quarters, instead of 400 quarters, his outlay for wages would be increased from 1600*l*. to 1700*l*., and his whole cost from 3000*l*. to 3100*l*. But the whole cost of the French manufacturer continues to be only 3030*l*. The English manufacturer, therefore, instead of possessing in the foreign market an advantage to the extent of one per cent. would now be undersold, and would be compelled, either to reduce the real wages of his labourers, or else to abandon the foreign trade, and throw them altogether out of work.

The illustrations now produced will be sufficient, it is hoped, to demonstrate the manner in which the high comparative value of food in this country, counteracts all our actual and acquired superiority in producing goods for the foreign market, and brings us so near to the verge of equality with our continental rivals, as to render it impossible that our operatives should obtain any material increase of price for the quantity of work which they perform. So long as the existing Corn Laws remain, so long will it be found impracticable, either to diminish the hours of labour, or to increase wages; and so long will every attempt to do either, inflict additional privation upon the working classes, by narrowing the foreign market, and contracting trade.

No measures for increasing the reward of labour can be successful, until the Corn Laws have been first abolished. Benevolent individuals, inattentive to the paralysing influence of these laws, have sought to improve the condition of the people by limiting the supply, and thereby increasing the value of labour; and with this view, have at one time recommended, that the labouring classes should reduce their numbers by a prudential abstinence from marriage; and, at another time, have urged them to obtain, either by Legislative enactment, or by combinations amongst themselves, a limitation of the hours of labour. Either of these modes of diminishing the supply of labour in the market, might have the effect of raising real wages, provided the natural and acquired superiority which England possesses in manufacturing industry, were not counteracted by the high comparative value of food. But while the Corn Laws continue to keep up the value of food, and to place us, in the foreign market, on the verge of equality with our continental competitors, neither these, nor any other conceivable measures, can have the effect of improving the condition of the operative classes. A reference to the preceding illustrations will immediately demonstrate this. While a French manufacturer, in producing a given quantity of goods, advances 1680*l.* for materials, machinery, and carriage, and 600 quarters of corn at 40*s.* per quarter, or 1200*l.*, for the wages of 300 men ; and while the English manufacturer, in producing the same quantity of goods, advances 1400*l.* for material, machinery, and carriage, and 400 quarters of corn at 80*s.*, or 1600*l.*, for the wages of 200 men ; a diminution in the supply, and increase in the price of labour, compelling him to add 25 quarters, or 100*l.*, to his advance for wages, would enable the French manufacturer, whom he had previously under-sold, to drive him out of the foreign market. It would signify nothing, from what cause the diminution in the supply, and rise in the price, of labour might proceed. Whether the reduction in the supply of labour were occasioned by a prudential abstinence from marriage, or by a combination for limiting the hours of work, the effect would be the same ; and the abortive attempt to force up wages beyond the artificial maximum created by the Corn Laws for enhancing the value of food, would terminate in the loss of employment, and in overwhelming calamity. Were food as cheap in England as it is in other manufacturing countries, it would be practicable to secure to the operative classes, in England, a higher rate of real wages *within the limit* of the superiority, which more efficacious labour, cheaper fuel and carriage, and better machinery, all contribute to confer upon England, in producing goods for the foreign market. But while the value of food in England is artificially raised above its value in those other manufacturing countries, which are our competitors in the foreign market, such an improvement in the rate of real wages is morally impossible. Until an alteration in the Corn Laws shall have secured us against foreign competition, all projects for raising wages will be found erroneous in principle, and ruinous in practice.

———

CHAPTER V.

ON MR. FIELDEN'S SCHEME FOR LIMITING THE HOURS OF LABOUR.

Mr. FIELDEN, the member for Oldham, in conjunction with the benevolent mono-maniac, Robert Owen, has propounded a plan for the benefit of the working classes, which it may not be improper or unuseful to examine. The plan is, that a universal combination shall be formed for limiting the hours of labour for adults, as well as for children, to eight hours a day ; and for securing to the work people, after the time of labour shall be thus reduced, the same wages which they now receive.

In explaining this plan, Mr. Fielden states, that " if the change were general, the lesser quantity " produced would command as much money as the " greater quantity now does ;" and that " those em- " ployed in factories, in making cloth, &c., would " only be able to procure three garments, or three " other things, after the advance, where they now " purchase four."

Here we have a singular inconsistency—nay, a palpable contradiction. The operatives are to receive the same wages as at present, while their wages are reduced one-fourth. The benefits they are to derive from the proposed combination amount to this, that, when the change becomes general, they shall get three garments, and three other things, where they now get four.

Mr. Fielden states, and states most correctly, that " our foreign trade resolves itself into barter;" and that, after the proposed plan shall be carried into effect, " the manufacturer will give to the " foreigner, and others, the same quantity of his " manufactures, for the same quantity of raw ma- " terials, as he now gives ; which quantity the " foreigner will have, or not continue to trade with " him." Mr. Fielden states these facts, to show that under the change he proposes, " we should not lose our foreign trade." But the facts, as he has himself stated them, lead to a directly opposite conclusion. It can be proved by the strictest demonstration—nay, it amounts very nearly to a self-evident proposition—that were the circumstances assumed by Mr. Fielden, really to occur, the foreign trade of England must be instantly suspended.

The facts assumed by Mr. Fielden are, that the combination to work only eight hours a day will diminish the quantity of goods one-fourth ; and that the diminished quantity will sell for the same price for which the larger quantity formerly sold ; so that if 400*l.* was formerly the price of 100 bales of any kind of goods, 400*l.* will be the price of 75 bales of the same goods. Now it must be apparent, upon a moment's consideration, that this extraordinary rise in the price of all British goods, would have the effect of arresting the export trade, and of prodigiously increasing the import trade. But if the export trade diminished, and the import trade increased, England would become indebted to other countries ; and, in order to balance her foreign accounts, money must be sent abroad, instead of goods. Now if money were, in this manner, sent abroad, the currency would be contracted, and prices would come down as rapidly as they had risen. But in what condition would the manufacturer now be placed ? He is obliged to pay the same money-wages to his labourers as before, while he receives, for the diminished quantity of goods which they produce, only three-fourths of the sum which he formerly received. His profit is turned into loss. He must leave off business, or become a bankrupt.

Let us show, by figures, in what manner the ruin of the manufacturer would be brought about. We will state his case in three different ways : 1*st.* before the hours of labour are reduced, as by the plan proposed ; 2*nd.* after the hours of labour have been reduced, and while the increased price of goods, assumed by Mr. Fielden, continues ; and, 3*rd.* after prices have fallen back to the original level from which they were raised.

I.

Case of the Manufacturer before the Reduction in the hours of labour.

EXPENDITURE.

Wages to 100 men working 12 hours   £. 2000
Fuel and machinery   -   -   1000
Raw materials   -   -   -   1000

Total expenditure   - £. 4000

RETURN.

1100 bales of goods, at 4*l.* per bale   £. 4400
Deduct expenditure   -   -   4000

Profit   -   -   -   400

II.

Case of the Manufacturer after the Reduction of the hours of labour from 12 *to* 8, *and while the diminished quantities of all goods sells for the same sum for which the undiminished quantities formerly sold.*

EXPENDITURE.

Wages to 100 men working 8 hours   £. 2000
Three-fourths of former fuel and
  machinery   -   -   -   1000
Three-fourths of former quantity of
  materials   -   -   -   1000

Total expenditure   - £. 4000

RETURN.

Three-fourths of former quantity of
goods, or 825 bales - - £.4400
Deduct expenditure - - 4000

Profit - - £. 400

III.

Case of the Manufacturer after the return of
Prices to their former level, and while he con-
tinues to pay full wages for 8 hours work.

EXPENDITURE.

Wages to 100 men working 8 hours £. 2000
Three-fourths the quantity of fuel
 and machinery employed in
 Case I. 750
Three-fourths former quantity of
 material used in Case I. - 750

Total expenditure - - £. 3500

RETURN.

Three-fourths of former quantity of
goods, or 825 bales - - £. 3300

Excess of expenditure, or dead loss £. 200

Thus we see, that it amounts to a strictly mathematical demonstration, that unless the prices of
all goods can be permanently raised, by the dimi-

nution of production, reducing the hours of labour by one-fourth, or from 12 to 8 hours, while wages remain unreduced, must occasion a loss to the manufacturer equivalent to one-fourth of the wages which he pays. If his profit had previously been just equal to one-fourth of the wages he advanced, this loss would absorb all profit; and if, as in practice must almost always be the case, his profits were less than one-fourth of the wages advanced, then the loss equivalent to one-fourth of his expenditure for wages, would not only absorb all profit, but would trench upon his capital.

All Mr. Fielden's arguments in support of his plan, turn upon the assumption, that prices will rise in the proportion in which production is diminished; but he has brought forward neither fact nor argument, to prove that foreign consumers would consent to purchase British manufactures, were five-and-twenty per cent. added to their present price. The continent of Europe, and the United States of North America can now manufacture *nearly* as cheap as England, and could manufacture much cheaper, were the prices of British goods increased by twenty-five per cent. Grant Mr. Fielden his assumption, that his plan would have the effect of raising the prices of British goods by five-and-twenty per cent., and it follows, as a necessary consequence, that, on the adoption of his plan, England must cease to be a manufacturing country. Deny his assumption, respecting the increase of prices, and equal ruin will be wrought, though in a somewhat different way. The merchant may in this case continue to sell British goods in the foreign market, until the destruction of the manufacturer puts an end to their production. This destruction, as we have already seen, would follow certainly and rapidly upon the adoption of a plan for compelling the manufacturer to pay the same money-wages as at present for working up a diminished quantity of goods, which he could not sell at advanced money-prices. Whether Mr. Fielden's assumption respecting the rise of prices be admitted, or denied, his project for diminishing production will be found equally impracticable, and equally ruinous.

Mr. Fielden tells us, and tells us most truly, that the foreigner will not continue to trade with us, unless we give him the same quantity of manufactures for the same quantity of raw material. But gold is a material produced in a foreign country; and on Mr. Fielden's own principle, the foreigner will not continue to deal with us, unless we give him the same quantity of manufactured goods for the same quantity of gold. Now, if goods and gold exchange in the same proportions as before, prices will be the same as before. Mr. Fielden, therefore, assumes two facts, which are at variance with, and destructive of, each other. If the foreigner *will not continue to give* us a greater quantity of material for the same quantity of goods, he will not give us a greater quantity of gold for the same quantity of goods. and prices will not rise; and if he *will continue to give* a greater quantity of gold for the same quantity of goods, so as to make prices rise, he will give a greater quantity of material for the same quantity of goods. Thus Mr. Fielden answers, and overthrows his own argument. When he tells us, and tells us truly, that foreign trade resolves itself into barter; and that the foreigner will not continue to deal with us, unless he obtain the same quantity of manufactures for the same quantity of material; he, by a necessary inference, also tells us, and tells us truly, that his assumption, respecting the rise of prices, is erroneous.

Mr. Fielden's motives, in endeavouring to aid the labouring classes in their laudable endeavours to improve their condition, entitle him to public approbation. But it is evident, that, in undertaking this momentous task, he has failed in making himself sufficiently acquainted with the causes which determine the real rate of wages in a manufacturing country extensively engaged in the business of supplying goods for the foreign market. If such a country does not possess peculiar advantages over the other manufacturing countries which are her competitors in the foreign market, it is morally impossible to secure for her operatives a higher rate of wages than that which prevails in the rival manufacturing countries. And on the other hand, if such a country does possess peculiar advantages in the fabrication of goods for the foreign market, then, within the limits of these advantages it becomes possible, under judicious arrangement, to render the wages of her operatives permanently higher than the wages obtained by the operatives of other countries. Now the plan proposed by Mr. Fielden, is not in conformity with these fundamental principles, but, on the contrary, is in direct opposition to them. One of the most considerable advantages which England possesses over other manufacturing countries, and which, if not counterbalanced by the high value of food, would enable her operatives to receive higher wages than the operatives of other countries, consists in that superior energy of labour, by which, as we have shown, a given number of labourers execute, within the year, a much greater quantity of work than the same number of labourers in other countries. This advantage, and this title to superior wages, the plan of Mr. Fielden goes to destroy. If the time of labour should be limited in England to eight hours a day, while on the continent it continues to be extended to 12 and 14 hours, no human power can save the operatives of England from the necessity of submitting to a lower rate of wages than that which the operatives of the continent receive. No candid man can deny that Mr. Fielden is, *in intention*, the friend of the working people ; but no lover of truth, acquainted with the causes which regulate the amount of wages, will hesitate to say, that, *in practice*, the plan which he has proposed for their adoption would lead them to destruction.

The operatives of England may obtain, under judicious arrangement, either a superior rate of wages, or a reduction in the hours of labour within the limits of the superiority, natural and acquired, which England possesses in supplying manufactured goods for the foreign market. This superiority consists in the greater quantity of work which an Englishman performs in a day or year, and in the greater cheapness of machinery, of fuel, and of carriage ; and this superiority is counteracted and limited, by the comparative dearness of food. No plan for improving the condition of the people can by possibility be effectual, unless it increases the quantity of work which can be executed in a day or year, or the *comparative* cheapness of machinery, fuel and carriage, or diminishes the *comparative* dearness of food. All projects for increasing wages, or for diminishing the hours of labour, which do not contain efficient provisions for accomplishing one or more of those objects, are founded in ignorance and in delusion, and must terminate in disappointment, and in aggravated distress. *The first step towards improvement must be the abolition of the Corn Laws.*

CHAPTER VI.

ON THE QUESTION, WOULD THE PROFITS
OF THE FARMER BE REDUCED BY SUCH
A REDUCTION IN THE VALUE OF FOOD, AS
WOULD ADMIT OF AN INCREASE OF REAL
WAGES ?

In manufacturing industry, the elementary cost
of production consists of food and raw material.
It therefore amounts to a self-evident proposition,
that, other things remaining the same, the profits
of the manufacturer must fall, as the value of
agricultural produce rises in relation to manufactured goods.   It is sometimes imagined, however, that this circumstance does not reduce
agricultural profits ; but that, on the contrary, an
increase in the value of raw produce is beneficial
to the farmer, in the same proportion in which it is
prejudicial to the manufacturer.   This is a fundamental error, and its prevalence amongst the
agricultural class, leads to the most mischievous
practical results.   In the long run, the interests
of the capitalist, who engages in agriculture, are
identical with the interests of the capitalist who
engages in manufactures.   The same causes which
raise or lower the rate of profit in one occupation,

raise or lower it in all. When rents are adjusted to the price of produce, a fall in the value of food and raw material, is as beneficial to the farmer, as to all other capitalists ; and a rise in their value, as injurious. These principles are so seldom acknowledged, and are of such vast practical importance, that it may be expedient briefly to demonstrate them. In endeavouring to do this, we will suppose, for the sake of avoiding complex details, that that part of productive expenditure which consists of wrought goods is represented by yards of cloth ; and that part which consists of raw produce, by quarters of corn. This will greatly simplify our proofs, without in any way impairing their conclusiveness.

CASE I.—In which a yard of cloth is equal in value to a quarter of corn.

MANUFACTURER ADVANCES

Food and raw material, equivalent to
  100 quarters of corn=100 yards of
  cloth   -   -   -   - 100 *yds.*
Clothing, furniture, and machinery,
  equivalent to 100 yards   -   - 100
                                            ———
                                            200
OBTAINS
Returns equivalent to 300 yards   - 300
                                            ———
Gains a profit of, being 50 upon his
  advances   -   -   - 100

FARMER ADVANCES

Food and seed=100 quarters of corn   100 *qrs.*
Clothing and furniture, equivalent
  to 100 suits of clothing = 100
  quarters   -   -   -   - 100
                                 —————
                                 200
                                 ═════

OBTAINS

A return of 400 quarters   -   - 400
                                 —————

Gross surplus of returns above advance 200
Pays as rent, 100 quarters   -   - 100
                                 —————

Nett surplus, or profit of 50 per cent.   100
                                 ═════

CASE II.—In which the increased value of agricultural produce, in relation to manufactured goods, causes one quarter of corn to be worth three yards of cloth.

MANUFACTURER ADVANCES

Food and raw material, equivalent to
  100 quarters=150 yards   - 150 *yds.*
Clothing, furniture, machinery,=100
  yards   -   -   -   - 100
                                   ———
                                 250

OBTAINS

Return, 300 yards - - -	300 *yds.*
Profit 20 per cent. upon advances -	50

FARMER ADVANCES

Food and seed=100 quarters -	100 *qrs.*
Clothing, implements, furniture	
=100 suits=66 quarters -	66
	166

OBTAINS

Produce, 400 quarters - -	400
Gross surplus - - -	234
Rent - - - -	201
Profit of 20 per cent. upon advance	
=166 quarters - -	33

In these two cases the capitals employed are identical. In both, the advances of the farmer, as well as those of the manufacturer, consist of agricultural produce equivalent to 100 quarters of corn, and of manufactured goods equivalent to

100 yards of cloth. When, as in Case I., a quarter of corn and a yard of cloth were of equal value, the rate of profit, both in agriculture and in manufactures, was 50 per cent.; because the farmer, as competition will always compel him to do, paid away, as rent, a portion of his produce sufficient to reduce the surplus remaining in his hands to an equality with the surplus realized by the manufacturer. When, as in Case II., the value of agricultural produce in relation to manufactured goods, rose 50 per cent., and two quarters of corn exchanged for three yards of cloth, then the rate of profit, as well in agriculture as in manufactures, fell from 50 to 20 per cent.; competition, as before, compelling the farmer to pay, as rent, all that portion of his surplus which exceeded the surplus gained by the manufacturer. In Case II., rent is raised from 100 to 201 quarters of corn; and, as by the supposition, the value of agricultural produce, in relation to manufactured goods, has risen 50 per cent., these 201 quarters will command in exchange $301\frac{1}{2}$ yards of cloth. Measured in corn, rent will be doubled; measured in cloth, it will appear to be trebled. The owner of the land will obtain an enormous advantage; but the advantage thus gained by the owner of land, so far from being beneficial to the farmer, will be obtained at his expense. The interest of the owner, and the interest of the cultivator of the soil, so far from being the same,

are directly opposed to each other. It can be shown by strictly mathematical demonstration, that an increase in the value of agricultural produce, raises the landlord's rent by reducing the farmer's profit.

When a rise takes place in the value of agricultural produce, the subsequent fall, which takes place in the farmer's profit, is occasioned by the competition which compels him to offer a higher rent. But when the farmer has a lease for a term of years, at a fixed rent, he is not immediately exposed to this competition; and, consequently, during the currency of his lease, the rise in the value of produce will be advantageous to him. Should the farmer, under the circumstances stated in Case I., have taken a lease at the fixed rent of 100 quarters of corn, then, when the value of his produce rose 50 per cent., as in Case II., his profit would not fall from 50 to 20 per cent.; but, on the contrary, would rise to 80 per cent. Because, advancing 100 quarters for seed and food, and 66 for clothing and implements, he obtains a gross return of 400 quarters. Out of this, he pays 100 quarters for rent, and has therefore, for his total advance of 166 quarters, a nett return of 300 quarters, being an increase of 80 per cent.

For the farmer, permanently, to retain a rate of return to his advances higher than that realized by other capitalists, would be morally impossible.

On the expiration of his lease, he would encounter competition; his profits would sink, not merely to their former level, but to that lower level now rendered general; and the rise in the value of agricultural produce, after conferring a temporary benefit upon the farmer, would fix him in a state of permanent depression.

By those who have not given sufficient attention to the important and fundamental principle, that, other things continuing the same, the ultimate effect of a rise in the value of agricultural produce, is, to raise the proprietor's rent, and to lower the farmer's profit, it may be supposed, perhaps, that the proof of this principle, presented in the preceding cases, is inconclusive; because the advances and return of the manufacturer are measured in cloth, and those of the farmer, in corn. It will be seen, however, that this difference in the measure makes no difference in the result. If we estimate the advances and the returns of the manufacturer in corn, or those of the farmer in cloth, the conclusion will come out the same. The vast—the incalculable, practical importance of the principle will justify us in resorting to further demonstrative details, in order to show that whether we employ cloth, or corn, or money, as our measure in estimating his advances and returns, a permanent rise in the value of agricultural produce, must have the effect, as leases expire, of reducing the cultivators' profit.

With respect to Case I., no error can by possibility result from estimating the advances and returns of the manufacturer in cloth, while those of the farmer are estimated in corn; because, a yard of cloth, and a quarter of corn, being of equal value, it is indifferent which is selected as the measure. With respect to Case II., however, in which two quarters of corn are equal in value to three yards of cloth, those not familiar with the principle, that a rise in the value of agricultural produce leads to a fall in agricultural profits, may entertain a suspicion, that, in adopting one measure for the manufacturer, and another for the farmer, some latent fallacy may be involved. To remove all doubt, as to the completeness of the proof of this most important principle, we will re-state Case II., measuring the advances and returns of the manufacturer in *corn*, and those of the farmer in *cloth*. It will be immediately perceived, that the results will be identical with those which were obtained when the measure for the manufacturer was *cloth*, and that for the farmer *corn*. Whatever may be the measure, the rate of profit, which was 50 per cent. when a quarter of corn and a yard of cloth were of equal value, will fall to 20 per cent. when two quarters become equivalent to three yards.

Case II.—repeated.

The Manufacturer *(measure changed from cloth to corn)*

ADVANCES

Food and raw material equivalent to
    100 quarters of corn   -   - 100 *qrs.*
Clothing and implements equal to 100
    yards of cloth$=66\frac{2}{3}$ quarters   - $66\frac{2}{3}$
                                        ————
        Total advance   -   - $166\frac{2}{3}$

OBTAINS

Return of 300 yards of cloth, equiva-
    lent to 200 quarters   -   - 200
                                        ————
Surplus of return, being 20 per cent.
    above the advance of $166\frac{2}{3}$ - $33\frac{1}{3}$
                                        ════

The Farmer *(measure changed from corn to cloth)*

ADVANCES

Food and seéd$=100$ quarters$=150$
    yards   -   -   -   150 *yds.*
Clothing and implements$=100$ yards   100
                                        ————
        Total advance   -   - 250

OBTAINS

Produce=400 quarters=600 yards - **600** *yds.*

Pays rent as before=200 quarters=
   300 yards   -   -   - 300

350

Retains nett surplus, being 20 per cent.
   upon his outlay of 250 yards   -   50

=====

The real cost of production, both in manufactures and in agriculture, consists of a certain quantity of manufactured goods, and of a certain quantity of agricultural produce. In estimating productive cost, and in comparing the capitalist's returns with his advances, we may employ as our measure, a given quantity either of wrought goods, or of raw produce. Measuring in kind, and by quantities, has some advantages over measuring by money value, inasmuch, as by the former method, we get rid of the complication arising from the considerations of currency and of price, and are enabled to perceive more immediately and distinctly the proportion in which the articles produced, exceed the articles expended in producing them. But measuring cost and reproduction in kind, though it may conduce to scientifical accuracy and precision, is yet liable to the objection of being less familiar to the general reader, than measuring in money. As in the present state of the country, there is no delusion more mischievous than the very prevalent one, that the high value of agricultural produce is beneficial to the farmer, it is expedient to demonstrate, under every possible form, the great practical truth, that a permanent rise in the value of agricultural produce, leads to a reduction in the rate of agricultural profit. With this view, the preceding cases are re-stated, with this difference, that money is employed as the measure of value, in estimating and composing the advances and returns.

In Case 1., when the manufactured goods, and agricultural produce consumed in production, are of equal value, we will assume that a yard of cloth, and a quarter of corn, sell for 40s. each ; and in Case II., when the increased demand for agricultural produce adds 50 per cent to its value, we will assume, that the price of a quarter of corn rises to 60s, while the price of a yard of cloth remains at 40s.

CASE I.—In which a yard of cloth, and a quarter of corn, sell each for 40s.

MANUFACTURER ADVANCES

Clothing, furniture, and machinery, equivalent to 100 yards of cloth, at 40s. per yard - - - £.200

Food and raw material, equivalent to 100 quarters of corn, at 40s. per quarter - - - 200

Total Expenditure - - £.400

OBTAINS

Finished articles, equivalent to 300
yards, at 40*s*. per yard -   -   *£*.600

Surplus or profit of 50 per cent.
upon his expenditure of *£*.400 - *£*.200

FARMER ADVANCES

Clothing, furniture, and implements,
equivalent to 100 yards of cloth,
at 40*s*. per yard   -   -   *£*.200
Food and seed, equivalent to 100
quarters of corn, at 40*s*. per
quarter -   -   -   -   200

Total Expenditure -   -   *£*.400

OBTAINS

Produce, equivalent to 400 quarters
of corn, at 40*s*. per quarter   -   *£*.800
Gross surplus, 200 quarters   -   400

Pays as rent, 100 quarters   -   200

Nett surplus, or profit, being 50 per
cent. upon expenditure -   -   *£*.200

CASE II.—In which the demand for agricultural produce raise the price of corn to 60s. per quarter, while the price of cloth remains at 40s. per yard.

MANUFACTURER ADVANCES

Clothing, furniture, and machinery, equivalent to 100 yards of cloth, at 40s. per yard - -	£.200
Food and raw material, equivalent to 100 quarters of corn, at 60s. per quarter - - -	300
Total advance - -	£.500

OBTAINS

Finished goods, equivalent to 300 yards of cloth, at 40s. per yard -	£.600
Profit, being 20 per cent. upon expenditure of £.500 - -	£.100

FARMER ADVANCES

Clothing and implements, equivalent to 100 yards of cloth, at 40s. per yard - - - -	£.200
Food and seed, equivalent to 100 quarters of corn, at 60s. per quarter - - - -	300
Total expenditure - -	£.500

OBTAINS

Produce equivalent to 400 quarters,
    at 60*s*. per quarter   -   - £.1200
                             ———

Gross surplus   -   -   - £.700
Pays as rent, 200 quarters -   -   600
                             ———

Nett surplus, being a profit of 20 per
    cent. upon the expenditure of £.500 £.100

Thus again we see, that whatever medium of measurement we employ, we arrive at the same inevitable conclusion, that a rise in the value of agricultural produce, is followed by a fall in agricultural profits, When the quantity of wrought goods obtained by the advance of a given quantity of raw produce, commands, in exchange, a less quantity of raw produce than before, it is self-evident that manufacturing profits must decline. Had the cultivators of the soil leases for ever, at unalterable rents, the same cause which depressed manufacturing, would raise agricultural profits, and the farmer would flourish amidst the general distress. But this is impossible. Throughout all the departments of industry, the rates of profit tend to a common level. When the quantity of manufactured goods prepared by the expenditure of a given quantity of agricultural produce, purchased a less quantity of such produce than before, the capital invested in manufactures would gain a less, while the capital invested in agriculture would obtain a 'greater, return than before. But as long as this difference in the rates of return to capital continued, so long would the competition for land be rendered more intense. The natural, the inevitable result would be, that tenants at will, and all other tenants, as their leases expired, would be compelled to pay, as rent, such an increased portion of their surplus produce, as would bring down agricultural profits to the reduced level of manufacturing profits. This, then, is the great practical conclusion with which all should be familiar. An increase in the value of agricultural produce, while it confers a temporary benefit upon farmers, protected against competition by a current lease, inflicts permanent injury and depression upon the important class who invest their capital in the cultivation of the soil.

A fall in the value of agricultural produce will, of course, be followed by effects the reverse of those occasioned by a rise. When the quantity of manufactured goods which is fabricated by the advance of a given quantity of food and materials, exchanges for a greater quantity of these articles of raw produce, then manufacturing profits become higher than before ; and when the quantity of agricultural produce, raised with the expenditure of a given quantity of clothing and implements, exchanges for a less quantity of these finished articles than before, then, it is self-evident, that agricultural profits will be lower than before. This, for a time, will occasion agricultural distress. But as the profits of the manufacturer increase, and those of the cultivator decline, there will be less competition for farms ; and tenants at will, and all other tenants, on the expiration of current leases, will demand, and must ultimately obtain, such a reduction of rents, as will leave in their hands a surplus produce, sufficient to raise agricultural profits, not merely to their former level, but to that higher level to which manufacturing profits may have risen. Thus, with respect to the effects of a fall in the value of agricultural produce, the important practical principles are, that such fall occasions temporary agricultural distress, while rents are in the course of adjustment to the reduced level ; and that, as this adjustment is effected, the fall in the value of produce confers upon those who invest capital in the cultivation of the soil, a permanent prosperity, greater than that which they previously enjoyed.

The principles above unfolded enable us to explain, with distinctness and precision, the causes of agricultural distress. When the price of agricultural produce fell, after the termination of the late war, there were two, and only two ways, by which a considerable fall in agricultural profits, and a diminution of agricultural capital might have been prevented ; namely, *first*, by an immediate reduction of money rents, and of other money charges upon land, in correspondence with the diminished price of produce; *secondly*, by such a reduction in the ancient standard of value, as would have perpetuated high nominal prices, and have been, in effect, the same thing as a reduction of rents, and of other fixed money charges. Had the landed proprietors of England, who then possessed the whole legislative power, adopted either of these courses, no fall of agricultural profits, no destruction of agricultural capital, could have occurred. They attempted neither. Unacquainted with the principles of economical science, and not possessing sufficient intelligence to perceive their own ignorance, the landed proprietors of that day became willing instruments, and co-operating agents, in working out their own destruction. If they chose to consent to measures for raising the value of the currency, they should, at the same time, have made a corresponding reduction in their own rents, and have compelled the Government to make a corresponding reduction in the public taxes. And, on the other hand, when they determined to keep up their own rents, and to support the minister in maintaining enormous establishments, they should have made it an indispensable condition, that the value of money should not be increased. But they seem to have acted under the influence of judicial blindness. They conceived, that without loss of profit, and destruction of capital, their tenants might continue to pay undiminished money rents, and money charges, in a currency enhanced in value; and, in order to render an impossibility possible, they clamoured for the Corn Laws, and, blind leaders of the blind, deluded their tenantry into the belief, that the farmer is benefited by high prices and high rents. This delusion, and the expectation that the Corn Laws would eventually restore prices, caused the necessary reduction in rents, and in other money charges, to be deferred. The consequences were, a ruinous fall in the rate of agricultural profit; the loss of agricultural capital; less perfect cultivation; the deterioration of the soil; the bankruptcy of tenants; the abandonment of land; the throwing out of labour; the all-absorbing increase of the poor's rate; and all that train of desolating evils, which, if the power of knowledge cannot now remove them, must speedily overwhelm labourer, farmer, and landlord, in one common ruin.

How different would have been the results had the landed proprietors, instead of clamouring for a Corn Law, and endeavouring to make food dear, adjusted rents, and other fixed money charges on the land, to the altered value of the currency, and reduced scale of prices. A reference to the preceding cases will demonstrate, that, had such an adjustment taken place, the consequence would have been, not a fall, but a rise in the rate of the farmer's profit. A corresponding rise of profits would have taken place in manufactures, and in trade. The superiority which England possesses in manufacturing industry, not being counterbalanced by a high comparative value of food, real wages might have been advanced, without incurring the danger of foreign competition. An absorbing poor rate would not have increased the cost of tilling, or have threatened to interdict the cultivation of the soil. A more numerous, and a more wealthy population, causing a more intense demand for building ground, for gardens, and for all those productions of the earth, which, from their bulk and perishable nature, cannot be imported, would have secured to the landed proprietors, a rental far exceeding that which it is possible to derive from farms employed in raising the main food of the people. But the effect of a free importation of food, in increasing the value of land, in a country possessing manufacturing superiority, has been shown in another place* ; and it is unnecessary to pursue the discussion, into which we have here digressed. Sufficient has been said for the present purpose, which is, to establish the principle, that an unrestricted importation of foreign corn, allowing of an increase of real wages, within the limits of our manufacturing superiority, could not have the effect of reducing the rate of the farmer's profit.

It is hoped that the proofs and illustrations inserted in the preceding pages, have established, beyond the possibility of doubt, the important practical truth, that farmers have no *permanent* interest in these restrictions on the

* *Essay on the External Corn Trade, Fourth Edition.—See also, a recent publication, entitled,* " England and America."

importation of foreign agricultural produce, which raise the price of food and raw materials. Farmers, who are under leases at a fixed money rent, have, no doubt, a *temporary* interest in high prices during the currency of these leases. But, in the long run, protecting duties, for raising the price of food, produce agricultural distress as certainly as they occasion manufacturing distress. Never was delusion more gross, than that which the proprietors of the soil practise upon their tenants, when they advise them to clamour for increased protection for the landed interest. When such advice is truly interpreted, it amounts just to this —" Aid us in enforcing arrangements which shall " have the effect of *raising our rents, and of* " *decreasing* your profits, and of rendering it " impossible to increase the real wages of labour, " without letting in foreign competition, and " throwing millions out of work."

CHAPTER VII.

ON THE QUESTION, WOULD A FREE TRADE IN CORN DIMINISH EMPLOYMENT, AND REDUCE WAGES, BY CONTRACTING THE HOME MARKET IN A GREATER PROPORTION THAN IT EXTENDED THE FOREIGN MARKET?

THE exclusive advocates, not of the *landed interest at large,* but of the *landed proprietors in particular,* endeavour to practise upon the manufacturers, a species of delusion similar to that which they have hitherto practised, too successfully, on the farmers. They contend, that the home market is better than the foreign market; and that importing corn, instead of purchasing it from the home grower, would be contracting the better, for the sake of extending the worse market. Were these advocates of the landed proprietors asked to explain what their meaning is, when they say that the home market is better than the foreign, it is possible that they might find some difficulty in giving an intelligible reply. It is essential, however, to correct inquiry, that the meaning of terms should be accurately fixed. In common discourse, the term, market, means *the place where commodities are sold;* in the language of commerce, the term expresses *the place where commodities find an effectual demand.* Now what is that effectual demand, the existence of which, in any particular place, constitutes a market, in the sense in which that term is employed in the language of commercial science. Effectual demand is simply this—the offer, in exchange for commodities, of that which will replace, with a surplus, or profit, that which is expended in reproducing them. Now, that which is expended in producing manufactured goods, is food and raw material. When, therefore, we speak of a market for manufactured goods, we speak of a place in which they will exchange for a greater quantity, or the price of a greater quantity, of food and raw material, than that which was expended in producing them. A good market for such goods, is a place where they will exchange for a quantity of food and material considerably greater than that expended in their production; and a bad market, is a place where they will exchange for a quantity of food and material little greater than their production cost. To tell the manufacturer that the home market is better than the foreign, when in the home market his goods exchange for a less quantity of food and material than in the foreign, is to assert a gross absurdity —a palpable contradiction.

With respect to effectual demand, it is important to bear in mind the distinction between its *extent* and its *intensity.* Effectual demand is *extensive,* in proportion to the quantity of commodities which can be sold at a price which will replace the cost of production with a surplus or profit, *whether that surplus be great or small.* Effectual demand is *intense*, in proportion as commodities sell at a price which replaces the cost of production with a large surplus, *whether the quantity of goods which can be thus sold be great or small.* It is plain that demand may be *extensive*, without being *intense;* and *intense*, without being *extensive.*

From what has been already said, it must be apparent, that when, by duties on the importation of agricultural produce, we increase the extent of the effectual demand of the home market, we must, by the self-same process, diminish its intensity. When the value of food and raw material is increased, in relation to wrought goods, such goods must sell at a price which replaces the elements of production with a less surplus than before; or, in other words, the intensity of the demand must be diminished. The extent of the demand measures the *amount of business;* the intensity of the demand measures the *rate of profit* at which busisiness may be done. The cultivation of inferior land, raising, in relation to his finished goods, the value of the manufacturer's elementary expenditure, can increase the amount of his transactions in the home market, only by reducing, at the same time, the rate of profit he is able to realize. Competition ever tends to bring profits to a common level. When the profits of the manufacturer who supplies the home market are brought down, those of the manufacturer who works for the foreign market, must speedily come down also.

The effects of the Corn Laws in lowering the rate of profit in a manufacturing country, would have been sufficiently obvious to reason, even if they had not been brought home to our senses by painful experience. One necessary and very injurious consequence of a fall in the rate of profit, is to throw small capitals out of employment, and to cause wealth to accumulate in a few hands. The middle classes are pressed down, and the extremes of opulence and of poverty rise in prominent contrast. When profits are high, fortunes are realized from small beginnings, and there is a constant bounty upon industry and frugality. But when profits are low, the stimulus of hope is withdrawn from those who are not born to wealth, and reckless indifference replaces persevering exertion. As profits fall, the capitalist is driven to press more and more heavily upon the operatives whom he employs. This is the worst effect of the Corn Laws, and of the low reward of industry which they occasion. A capitalist, we will suppose, pays 1000*l.* in wages, and 1000*l.* for materials, and gets a finished article, which he sells for 2200*l.* But the 200*l.*, thus gained upon his advances, for wages and materials, is insufficient to pay the rent of his buildings, and the wear and tear of his machines, and he perceives that he must either do better, or give up his business. Now in what way can he do better? He cannot get more for his goods—

he cannot get his materials for less—and he cannot do without buildings and machines. He therefore goes to the operative, and says, I cannot employ you on the same terms as before; you must consent to take less wages, or to work a greater number of hours.

When a low rate of profit predisposes industry to periodical paroxysms of distress, it will not unfrequently occur, that though wages have come down to the starving point, and though the hours of work have been extended to the utmost limits of human endurance, yet the finished article will not sell at a price which will replace its cost. It is obviously impossible that this should long continue. What then can be done? new machinery is resorted to, which neither eats nor tires, and thus human labour is supplanted by mechanical power. There can be no doubt that the Corn Laws have caused machinery to be employed in this country more extensively than it otherwise would have been. When the price of provisions is low, human labour may be cheaper than mechanical power. But as food becomes dear, the machine, which does not eat, will become less costly than the operative, who must be fed while at work. In many branches of trade, it is the price of corn which determines whether machinery can be advantageously introduced or not. Other things remaining the same, as the value of food is raised, mechanical power will be brought more and more into competition with human labour; and the operative will be employed at wages reduced to the starving point, and for the longest period of time which nature can endure.

This is the state of things to which we are rapidly approaching ; the state of things at which, in some of the principal seats of industry, we already have arrived. The condition of the working people is at once distressing and alarming, and demands the immediate attention of the Legislature. Parliament cannot compel the capitalist to carry on his business at a loss. It is both morally and physically impossible, that production should be long continued, when its expenses cease to be replaced. As the value of raw produce rises in relation to wrought goods, we at length arrive at the point at which the finished article ceases to be worth the food and material which, in the previous state of wages, were consumed in preparing it. When things have been brought to this pass, the operative has but one alternative : he must either do more work for the same wages, or else be thrown altogether out of employment. No combination, no bill, for regulating the hours of labour, can, by possibility, relieve him from this hard necessity.

Has Parliament, then, no power to relieve the people from the distress which overwhelms them ? Yes : it has the power to go at once to the root of the evil, and to remove entirely the cause of the disease. Parliament has power to abolish the Corn Laws, and to open a free trade with those countries which, having vast regions of fertile territory yet to reclaim, can, with the greatest advantage to themselves, give us cheap raw produce in exchange for our wrought goods. This is that which would relieve the people. No other remedy can eradicate the national disease.

Russia, and the United States of North America, are the principal countries with which a free trade, consisting of the interchange of wrought goods for raw produce, can be established. To regulate the trade with these countries upon the principles of reciprocity and freedom, is the main object to which the attention of the Legislature should be directed. To its attainment, no insuperable, no serious difficulty is opposed. It is the obvious, the decided interest of Russia, and of the United States, to establish with England commercial relations, founded on these principles. Giving raw produce for wrought goods, a species of trade which would impoverish and depopulate France, would impart additional momentum to the progress of Russia and America ; and, rapid as the advance of these great countries hitherto has been, would render it, in future, more rapid still.

Where abundance of new and fertile land remains to be resorted to, the cause of retardation is, the difficulty of working up the raw produce of the soil. This cause of retardation, free trade with a manufacturing country immediately removes. If, in a remote and thinly-peopled district of Russia, 100 men raised food for 300, while it required 200 men to make clothing for 300, then as the labour of 300 would do no more than just replace the food and clothing consumed by 300, industry would be suspended ; for the simple reason, that it could realize no profit. But were the food raised in Russia by 100 men sent to England, and were clothing for 300 brought back in exchange, then in Russia the advance of food and clothing for 200 would bring a return of food and clothing for 300 ; and the profits of agriculture, which before were nothing, would, through the intervention of commerce, become 50 per cent.

Thus, in urging Russia to establish with England an unfettered and reciprocal trade, we can prove to her, by reasoning strictly demonstrative, that, by adopting this liberal policy, she would obtain for herself the most decisive advantage. But, lest the prospect of advantage should be insufficient to induce her to depart from established usage, we ought at the same time to quicken her apprehension, by the fear of loss. With this view, while we propose to take off the import duties upon the corn, and tallow, and hides, produced in the dominions of Russia, on the condition that Russia should remit her duties upon the importation of British goods, we should at the same time distinctly inform her, that if she persists in enforcing her tariff against us, we shall not only retain our existing import duties upon the products of the Russian territory, but will reimpose, as respects Russia, the duty upon hemp, prema-

turely taken off by the last Parliament, while we
receive, duty free, the corn, and hemp, and tallow,
and hides, from all other countries, consenting to
a more liberal commercial code. This mode of
proceeding would be effectual. The hope of obtaining a more extended export trade to England,
combined with the fear of throwing into the hands
of other countries a part of that which she now
enjoys, would constrain Russia to lower her tariff
in favour of our manufactured goods. We know,
by repeated experience, that the Russian government, despotic though it be, dare not offend the
great proprietors of the soil, by risking that export
trade to England, upon which their revenue prin-
cipally depends. On one occasion, when the
autocrat interdicted the exportation of hemp, and
other naval stores to England, he paid for his
temerity the forfeit of his life. And at a later
period, it was the national resentment kindled in
Russia, by the interruption of commerce, which
gave birth to the grand effort against France, then
apparently irresistible, which ended in the down-
fall of Napoleon.

There can exist no doubt but that, by a tem-
perate, firm, and judicious enforcement of the
principle of reciprocity, we may succeed in esta-
blishing with Russia a trade free on both sides,
and consisting of the interchange of wrought goods
and raw produce. The advantages of such a trade
it would be difficult to estimate. As cultivation
extended over the vast regions of the Russian

empire, the market for British fabrics would perpetually expand. Who can calculate what the *extent* and the *intensity* of demand might become, as canals and rail-roads conveyed food and raw materials, from remote interior regions, to all the navigable streams falling into the Baltic and the Black Sea; and thus enabled the British manufacturer to replace, at decreasing cost, the elements of his productive capital.

It may be thought that this is drawing too largely on the future; and that, with respect to Russia, the day is yet far distant when such improvements can be realized. Be it so, with respect to Russia. With respect to the United States, the day is not distant—it is now at hand—it already has arrived. In that country of the free, there is a population of twelve millions, doubling in a period of about five-and-twenty years. The mean annual increase is upwards of half a million of souls; and of this increase, the greater portion spreads over the unreclaimed lands of the western territory. Here the forest recedes before them; towns and villages rise up as by enchantment; and the tide of agricultural improvement, and of Christian civilization, flows with still increasing velocity, from the shores of the Atlantic towards those of the Pacific.

Let us descend from generals to particulars. We find, from an inspection of the documents accompanying the President's message to Congress, that it is stated, in the report of the Commissioners of the General Land Office, that the quantity of land purchased from individuals by the Government, during the year 1826, was 1,274,644 acres. Some years prior to this, the lands in the Genesee country, now forming the State of Ohio, were purchased from the United States for about 3*s*. an acre, though, at the period of the purchase, there was scarcely a christian inhabitant throughout the whole district. In 1821, however, the population of the State of Ohio amounted to 500,000 souls; since that period, hundreds of thousands have passed into other new states, founded still further westward; and now throughout the vast regions of the Ohio, the Wabash, the Missouri, and Mississippi, cultivation is spreading with miraculous rapidity. Here, there is a market in which, for generations, the demand for wrought goods must increase both in extent and in intensity. The valley of the Mississippi, 1400 miles in length, and nearly the same in breadth, and intersected throughout all its vast extent by navigable streams, is itself capable of supplying food and raw material for a population greater than that of the whole of Europe. When the landed proprietors urge the merchants and manufacturers, to prefer the home to the foreign market, their language, truly interpreted, amounts to this, "Aid us in " raising the value of your food and raw ma- " terials, and in excluding you from markets of " incalculable extent, in order that we, the lords " of the soil, may keep up the rents of land, and

" keep down the profits of trade, and the wages
" of labour."

Never before, in the history of the world, had
any two countries so vast and extraordinary a
power of promoting the prosperity of each other,
as that possessed by England and the United
States. Each has an unlimited command over
that, which, in the peculiar circumstances of the
other, is the one thing needful. With however
small a proportion of his labour, the agriculturist
may be able to raise the food and seed consumed
in cultivation, if it require a *large* proportion of
his produce, to replace his clothing and implements, the surplus or profit cannot be great.
And, on the other hand, with however *small* a
portion of labour, the manufacturer can work up
the clothing and machinery he expends, if it
requires a *great* proportion of his finished articles,
to replace food and material, profit will be reduced
to the lowest rate at which business can be carried
on, and wages will sink to the starving point. In
the agricultural regions of America, prosperity is
less rapid than it otherwise might be, because the
value of raw produce is low, in relation to wrought
goods; while, in the manufacturing districts of
England distress prevails, because the value of
wrought goods is low, in relation to food and
material. Were the manufactures of England
admitted duty free into America, prosperity would
be there accelerated; and were the agricultural
produce of America admitted duty free into Eng-

land, the cause of the pressure upon the people would be removed, and the reward of labour might become as ample as it is in the United States of North America.

Never before, in the history of the world, did any two countries possess, in so extraordinary a degree, the power of promoting the prosperity of each other; and never before, in the annals of human folly, was there so melancholy an example " of the small portion of wisdom which governs nations," as that exhibited by England and the United States, in refusing to receive from each other the inestimable gifts which an unrestricted commercial intercourse would have brought. In this race of wretched absurdity, America was outstripped by England. The tariff rulers of the United States, in checking the importation of manufactured goods, have lowered profits, and retarded prosperity; while the borough oligarchy of England, in excluding foreign agricultural produce, have not only plundered the capitalist, but have brought some portions of the working classes to the verge of starvation. But in both countries a better system is approaching—a great and beneficial change is at hand. The southern states of the American Union will no longer submit to be plundered by the tariff; and now that the great manufacturing towns of England are represented in Parliament, they will no longer submit to be plundered by the Corn Laws.

The abolition of the Corn Laws, is the great

measure of national relief, which the people should demand, and which the Parliament should adopt. Were the hours of labour reduced, without a reduction in the value of food, either profits or wages, or both, must come down. But can the master manufacturer go on, if profits fall? Can the operative live, if wages are reduced? These are questions of fearful import. If industry be not relieved by reducing the value of raw produce in relation to wrought goods, it will require no spirit of prophecy to predict the calamitous result. We shall have first, a distressing stagnation of trade, and then a terrific convulsion. While there is yet time to avert the danger, let masters and operatives, instead of engaging in ruinous contests with each other, unite in petitioning the Legislature for the immediate commencement of that reform in our commercial policy, without which the distress of the people cannot be relieved, nor the peace of the country preserved.

F I N I S.